# THE
# donut

*HISTORY, RECIPES, AND LORE*

*from*

*BOSTON to BERLIN*

## MICHAEL KRONDL

CHICAGO
REVIEW
PRESS

Copyright © 2014 by Michael Krondl
First edition
Published by Chicago Review Press, Incorporated
814 North Franklin Street
Chicago, Illinois 60610
ISBN 978-1-61374-670-7

Library of Congress Cataloging-in-Publication Data
Krondl, Michael.
 The donut : history, recipes, and lore from Boston to Berlin / Michael Krondl. — First edition.
     pages cm
 Includes bibliographical references and index.
 ISBN 978-1-61374-670-7 (trade paper)
1. Doughnuts—History. I. Title.

TX770.D67K76 2014
641.86'53—dc23
                                    2013040685

Cover design: Natalya Balnova
Cover photograph: Direct Digital Photography
Interior design: Jonathan Hahn
Interior art credits: Selected item(s) found in this book are from the Gerald W. Williams Collection,
Special Collections & Archives Research Center, Oregon State University

Printed in the United States of America
5  4  3  2  1

# CONTENTS

# DONUT RECIPES

"Doughnuts are real food for real people."
—*Fleischman's Recipes* (1920)

# INTRODUCTION

## *HEAVEN AND HELL*

*D*oes this sound familiar? You're asleep at your desk, dreaming of fashion models dressed as raspberry cream donuts parading their stuff down a narrow runway, the chocolate icing glistening in the spotlights. Then, without warning, dream turns to nightmare. Harsh reality jolts you to your senses. You startle awake, only to find that the box of donuts that inspired your fantasy and gave meaning to your day sits empty, barren, denuded of all but the most pathetic crumbs. In a panic, you scramble for the emergency donut hidden in a hollowed-out emergency manual. But it's gone. Under the circumstances, who wouldn't sell their soul to the devil for a donut?

It worked for Homer Simpson. Faster than you can say "honey-dipped old-fashioned," the devil showed up, a contract in one hand and a big, beautiful donut, practically glowing with luscious pink icing, in the other. OK, I realize this sort of thing doesn't happen every day. In Homer's case, he had to wait for the *Simpsons'* fifth-season Halloween special. And I understand that it may be trickier if you aren't a cartoon character. Not all of us have Marge to back us up. In the episode, the good-hearted, blue-haired homemaker has no trouble sweet-talking an infernal jury into releasing her doughboy of a husband from the devil's grip. After a short sojourn in hell, Homer is reunited with his family and all's well that ends well—well, sort of. As punishment for outsmarting Satan, Homer wakes up the next day with his head a donut, which wouldn't be so bad except that his house is now surrounded by Springfield's finest, armed with coffee mugs and primed for a little donut action.

Matt Groening says that he made Homer a donut junkie because the cartoonist's father's favorite dessert was a donut. (Groening also named the character after his father.) But I figure there's got to be more to it than that. Homer is kind of like a donut: lumpy, lovable, and not altogether good for you. Like the hero of Springfield, the donut embodies the everyday Joe, the cop on the beat, the bus driver, the guy working the assembly line.

In both World Wars, American soldiers were glad for a taste of home, especially when it came in the form of a fried dough ring.

We're all a lot more like Homer than we'd care to admit, at least when it comes to fried pastry rings. Like the citizens of the fictional Springfield, real-life Americans share the knowledge that eating too many donuts will send you straight to hell; but neither group seems to give a damn.

Indulgence (just another word for sin) or pleasure (ditto) has long been associated with donuts. In many Catholic countries, donuts were what you ate during carnival in between getting drunk, cross-dressing, cheating on your wife, running off with your boy toy, or knifing your enemies. After all, if you had to spend all of Lent repenting, you might as well have something to repent for.

Yet that barely scratches the icing when it comes to the deep significance of donuts. With a history that goes back at least a couple thousand years, fried dough balls have meant lots of things to lots of people. In medieval India, they could be a quick pick-me-up between bouts of royal lovemaking. Five thousand miles away, in old Vienna, sharing a donut with your girlfriend practically meant you were engaged. Not that donuts were always sinful. Among many Jews they're the traditional food for Hanukkah; for most Muslims fried treats are mandatory for Ramadan. In American culture, their meaning has shifted over the years. In the nineteenth century, they were considered very much a New England specialty, so much so that before Yankee volunteers marched off to the Civil War, their stomachs were stuffed with fried dough. In the twentieth century, the donut became the all-American pastry. Assuring a steady supply at the front was considered essential to the war effort in both World Wars. To American GIs, the holey pastries were a kind of calling card from home, reminding them of what they were fighting for.

Back in nineteenth-century America, donuts used to be a homemade treat, lovingly cut by mom into diamonds and squares, in little "nuts" and large rings, but almost always cooked in kettles of lard. It was a dangerous proposition, especially in the early days when the kettle was hanging over an open fire. Then in the twentieth century, donut-hungry engineers came up with contraptions to automate the donut-making process. Next thing you know, fresh sinkers could be had morning, noon, and night in every state of the union. I'd argue that it was donuts, not burgers, that started the whole fast-food chain thing. (They certainly did it better; I'll take a Krispy Kreme over a Big Mac any day.) At any rate, donuts became something you bought at the corner shop. Instead of Mom being associated with hot, freshly made donuts, she came to be linked with Rice Krispies treats and Duncan Hines. If you were lucky, she'd pick up a dozen at Dunkin' Donuts on her way home from her nine to five.

Today, donuts are once again on the rise, with donut chefs cooking up organic and vegan and locally sourced versions of the old-fashioned glazed. They've gone nuts with the flavors: fancy a pistachio version or perhaps one flavored with marzipan or a jelly-filled donut with a peanut butter glaze? Maybe the term *donut connoisseur* isn't such an oxymoron anymore.

With so many to choose from, it's perhaps worth explaining what I mean by the word *donut*, other than just defining it as a fried lump of happiness. Obviously it qualifies if it's sweet, cooked in fat, and shaped like a donut—or a torus if you were paying attention in math class. However as any Dunkin' Donuts counter person is surely eager to explain, donut geometry is not limited to the torus. We also have our oblate spheroids, aka jelly donuts; our mini spheroids—that is, donut holes; and our Mobius strips, better known as French crullers. Some years back, Dunkin' Donuts gave up making regular crullers, which apparently defy the geometric aptitude of their machinery, but surely that doesn't make them any less of a donut.

And let's not forget all those fried dough balls that you won't find in a normal American donut shop: New Orleans's beignets, East L.A.'s churros, or the hot and greasy zeppole of New York's San Gennaro street festival. Surely they qualify as donuts even if their wacky contours defy mathematical formula.

Every culture that has figured out that fat and sugar taste good has cooked up some version of the donut. Does that mean a desire for donuts is hardwired into our genes? Or is fried dough an acquired taste, like pickled herring or Spam? In other words, is it nature or nurture? If you're of the scientific bent, this is more difficult to prove than you might initially think. It's no picnic trying to find a large-enough group of donut virgins to carry out your research. For his 1984 study, University of Michigan professor Christian S. Crandall had to trek to a remote Alaskan fishing village to find subjects for his donut inquiry. The experiment, as documented in the *Journal of Social Psychology*, was essentially this: some 225 people at a local cannery were exposed to a constant quantity of stimuli (donuts) for thirteen out of twenty-nine days. Apparently the stimuli were all of the cake variety; however, the subjects could choose from a variety of toppings, which included white and chocolate icing, flaked coconut, chopped nuts, and cinnamon sugar. After a careful tabulation of the results, the researchers had the data they needed to publish their results. "An increased rate of consumption of doughnuts in a free-feeding situation," Professor Crandall writes in the paper, "corresponded to the number of trials subjects had with the food." Which is to say, the more donuts they ate, the more donuts they wanted. Isn't science grand!

Whether the cause is nature or nurture, the free-feeding situation available to us in the United States means we consume billions of donuts each year. Market researchers tell us that our favorite stimuli are glazed, followed by yeast donuts, donut holes, cake donuts, and filled donuts.

Personally, I'm pretty eclectic in my donut tastes. But I guess I knew I'd have to be when I embarked on this project. I also feel a certain affinity to Dr. Crandall (and it isn't

## DONUTS VS. DOUGHNUTS

There seems to be no consensus about whether to spell the word with or without the *ugh*. Originally the sweet snack was named a *dough nut* because that's what it looked like: a walnut-sized lump of fried dough. Then, in the early eighteen hundreds, this was contracted into *doughnut*, around the same time as the pastry developed its distinctive ring shape. In transcriptions of colloquial American speech in the post–Civil War era, the word was soon shrunk to *donut*. After the First World War, this Americanized spelling was popularized in ads by Dono and other early donut companies. Today, the shorter form is preferred three to one (at least according to Google), and who am I to buck the crowd? In the following pages, you'll notice I stick to *donut* unless I'm quoting somebody else.

just that our names are pronounced the same). Like him, I've been required to do a little traveling and found it necessary to tabulate the results. I had to visit Seattle, not only to compare and contrast Top Pot's risen and cake donuts (toothsome and light in the first case and crumbling and tender in the second) but also to check out the warm-from-the-fryer mini donuts sold at a little stand in the Pike Place Market (a little overhyped I decided after eating a half dozen of the plain and three or four of the bacon-topped variety). Naturally, I had to analyze the qualitative difference between the scrumptious Austrian apricot jam–filled donuts in Vienna and the yeast-raised pillows filled with luscious vanilla cream that you get in Venice (I found the taste differential within the statistical margin of error). My data indicates that the sugar-dusted puffs Parisians call *beignets soufflés* are measurably lighter than the meltingly soft and cakey red velvet donuts they sell at the Peter Pan bakery in Brooklyn, but 37 percent less fun to dunk. I think that Professor Crandall would be gratified to hear that I have replicated his results, and indeed the more donuts you eat, the more you want. Like him, I feel that in my own small way, I've contributed to the stock of human knowledge. And I didn't even have to sell my soul to the devil (unless there's something my agent isn't telling me).

# 1

# THE HOLY DONUT

## NUN'S FARTS

People love telling stories about food, and the more improbable the better. Certainly a complete absence of corroborating evidence never seems to get in the way. Take nun's farts, for example. This fritter, called *pet de nonne* in French, is an airy mouthful of crisp-tender dough, often thickly dusted with powdered sugar. The name goes back hundreds of years. As the eighteenth-century French author of *In Praise of the Fart: A Dissertation on Its Historical, Anatomical, Philosophical Origin, on Its Antiquity and Virtues* explained, this is a kind of globe-shaped fritter. He neglects to add that it is typically made by frying cream puff dough. As far as the name? "It was the nuns themselves who gave the name fart to one of their most exquisite pastries," he writes. "Everyone knows nun's farts, of which the [spiritual] directors, abbots, priests, and prelates are so fond and always well supplied."

As time passed, the story was fleshed out. Writing some one hundred years later, French food writer Jean-Camille Fulbert-Dumonteil painted a much more detailed picture. "On the banks of the Loire, beneath the sweet skies of Touraine rises the ancient Abbey of Marmoutier," the nun fart chronicler begins his account, without identifying just when the incident in question was supposed to have taken place. Apparently the abbess of that bygone era was known as quite the foodie ("neither the sky nor cuisine held any secrets for her"), and as a result the place was overrun by pilgrims looking for a three-star meal. The nuns knew they had a good thing going. "If God came down to earth in search of a good meal, he'd come to Marmoutier," they confessed.

One unspecified year, on the great festival day of St. Martin, the abbey was packed with even more hungry friars than usual, all presided over by the Archbishop of Tours. Not wishing to disappoint the great prelate, the nuns leaped into a whirlwind of activity to assemble a feast worthy of the occasion. Exquisite ragouts bubbled on the stoves. Fat capons, chickens, quail, and rabbits spun before roaring fires. The aromas of vanilla, citron, orange, nutmeg, cinnamon, and orange-flower water wafted throughout the vast kitchen. In preparation for the feast, the abbess herself stood before a great cauldron of boiling fat with Agnes, her favorite young nun, at her side, preparing to fry a batch of her signature fritters. Dumonteil informs us that the novice was not only a paragon of every nunnish virtue, but she could cook too. ("To her exceptional merits were joined the most marvelous culinary abilities.")

As the demure Agnes stood at the abbess's side, balancing a ball of the dough on her delicate spoon, out of nowhere ("ô scandale") came a strange, resonant, rhythmic, and prolonged sound, like the groan of an organ. The eyes of every mortified nun searched to see what could be the source of this woeful noise, and all eventually fixed on poor Agnes. Our virginal novice turned ashen white, then strawberry red, and, finally, trembling with shame, she dropped the morsel of dough into the hot grease. Astonishingly—nay miraculously!— the morsel enlarged, turned golden brown and engorged into a globe. The nuns gathered round to taste this new child of culinary providence and pronounced it wondrous. And the name? Well, was there any other choice?

Even if Dumonteil's story is delightfully implausible, at least it's not impossible. Unlike a description given by the *Encyclopaedia Londinensis* in 1823, which explains that the pastry is made by having the cook use a tube to blow into the batter in the manner of soap bubbles. (In real life, the way choux pastry works is that the airy center is formed when trapped steam expands the pastry even as the outside crust hardens to trap the air within.) But the *Encyclopaedia*'s Protestant author was too busy making an ideological point about these papist trifles to worry himself with facts. As far as he was concerned, the presence of nun's farts on his side of the channel was just one more sign that England had run out of wind: "No wonder that our finical gentry should be so loose in their principles, as well as weak in their bodies, when the solid substantial protestant mince-pie has given place among them to the Roman catholic amulets, and to the light, puffy, heterodox, *pets de [nonnes]*."

Needless to say, despite the story about their miraculous lineage, nun's farts most likely have a less saintly origin. According to that oracle of the French language, the dictionary of the Academie française, before the nuns came into the picture, there were *pets de putain* (whore's farts), which were, in turn, preceded by medieval *pets d'Espagne* (Spanish farts). The late-fourteenth-century account books of Margaret of Flanders mention not only the Spanish variety but also those belonging to gentlemen (*pets chevalier*).

The trouble is that we don't have any recipes for either those early Spanish or gentlemanly exhalations. The earliest instructions on how to make these sorts of airy crullers come from Italy, though with names that cry out for a little French *fantasie*. A sixteenth-century papal chef calls his fried miracles merely *frittelle alla Veneziana*, Venetian fritters. They still make them there for Carnival, so if you happen to be in town, seek them out. They're heavenly.

## THE PREHISTORY OF THE DONUT

The story of donuts not only precedes the tale of the precocious nun but even Christianity itself. In fact it's likely that fried dough has been around ever since people first learned about the culinary potential of hot grease. A three-thousand-year-old inscription from the time of Pharaoh Ramses III seems to show a couple of cooks deep-frying strips of dough in a pot set over a fire. A millennium later, the Greeks certainly had something I'd call a donut. Athenaeus, the ancient world's best-known food maven, mentions at least a couple of donut-like treats. In a book called the *Deipnosophists* (*Banquet of the Learned*), the Greek author assembles a fictional toga party of learned scholars to chew the fat on everything from the proper way of cooking cuttlefish to the benefits of gay sex. "I am fond of cakes," the narrator declares before launching into a heavily annotated compendium that goes on for pages. In the midst of this exhaustive tour of cheesecakes, nut confections, and other sweetmeats, our guide points out two sorts of fried cakes. First he singles out something called fried bread, which may or may not be sweet. But then he goes on to describe *enkrides*. This delicate morsel of fried dough dripping with honey sounds an awful lot like what contemporary Greeks call *loukoumades.* "[It is] a small pastry deep-fried in olive oil and covered with honey afterward," our learned donut authority explains, making sure to reference some half dozen literary sources who mention this classical cruller.

The Romans had fried dough balls too. The curmudgeonly third century BCE statesman Cato the Elder had no use for the trendy indulgences of a younger generation, but he wasn't against all worldly pleasures. He was fond enough of his *globi* (balls) to write down the recipe. These ball-shaped fritters were made by mixing together equal parts of fresh cheese and spelt flour. They were fried until crisp and caramelized on the outside before being dipped in honey and sprinkled with poppy seeds. They sound utterly delicious. A few centuries later, the Roman cookbook writer known as Apicius gives us a very different fried-dough recipe. This one is made using a method resembling the one used to make today's churros. To make the dough, you boil water or milk with flour. Apicius then has you cool and cut it in pieces before frying in olive oil. Puffed and crunchy from the hot oil, the fritters were drizzled with honey before serving. Interestingly, in Naples, the traditional method of making the dough for zeppole is almost identical.

One thing these ancient sources don't mention is any connection between fried cakes and religion, something that you find over and over in many other fry-happy cultures. According to some readings of Leviticus, a text that scholars date back at least twenty-five hundred years, worshippers were instructed to bring an offering of "cakes mingled with oil, of fine flour, fried"—as the King James Bible translates it. Sounds like donuts, right? Sure, until the biblical nitpickers get a hold of it, and then you get a dozen dueling opinions about what the original text really means. Depending on the authority, that ranges from a kind of greasy matzo all the way to a shallow-fried donut and every variation in between. God knows, I'm not getting in the middle of that food fight.

The connection between fried dough and Hanukkah is much less controversial. If you know anything about the Jewish festival of lights, you've probably heard of potato latkes, but if you think these reflect some age-old Hebrew tradition, think again. Potatoes didn't even make it to the Jewish settlements in Eastern Europe until the eighteenth century. The point of the pancakes isn't the potatoes, it's the fact that they're fried. That's why other Jewish communities put donuts on the holiday menu.

Hanukkah celebrates a miracle that was supposed to have taken place some twenty-two hundred years ago in the Holy Land. After a devastating war, Jerusalem was a wreck, its temple desecrated, and Judaism itself outlawed in its own homeland. But the Jews fought back and, led by the priestly family of the Maccabees, recaptured Jerusalem, the temple, the whole lot. But there was a problem. Once they'd rededicated the temple, all they could find was one little vial of the ritually untainted olive oil needed for the nine-branched candelabra, barely enough to keep the thing going for a single day. And here's where the miracle comes in, because for eight days and nights, it burned on and on. Or at least that's the way the writers of the Talmud told it—some five hundred years later. In years to come Jews would commemorate the miracle by lighting a menorah for the holiday and, at least since the Middle Ages, they have found it a convenient excuse to fry dough. The miracle involved oil, right? So what do you do with oil? You use it to fry donuts!

The shape and names of these Hanukkah sinkers vary from place to place. If your heritage is Sephardic, you'll call them *bimuelos,* and if your family comes from Syria, *zalabia*. In Morocco, they go in for a fritter resembling an Amish funnel cake. Other North African Jews roll cookie dough into a rose shape before frying and dipping it in sugar syrup or honey. Even in India, Jews turn to a local fried specialty, *gulab jamun*, for the festival. And to make sure everyone is included in this fry fest, many Sephardic Jews distribute their fritters to those who are less donut endowed.

Perhaps in time people in the Middle East will realize how much they have in common. For example, Turkish Jews fry up *lokmas* for Hanukkah. Both the name and the recipe come from the Arabic *luqmat al-qadi*—meaning "judge's morsels." (Greek loukoumades share the same etymology.) Muslims and Jews alike make these fritters by dropping balls of yeast batter into hot oil before dipping them in a rosewater-scented syrup. The resulting sweet, aromatic mouthfuls are disarmingly both crisp and moist. In the old days, the recipes could be more complex. A version from medieval Baghdad ups the ante by adding a filling of almond paste. Those medieval judges were not fools.

There are dozens of fried desserts across the Muslim world. Some resemble fried cookies while others are more donut-like. Morocco's *sfenj* looks just like an American old-fashioned, hole and all. Given all the fuss, expense, and bother of making fried dough, these are usually

In Algeria, *zalabia* takes the form of long batons, made with a light, crispy yeast batter, which, when fried, is briefly dipped in syrup.

the treats are called there. Reporting from the Algerian town of Boufarik in 2010, local correspondent Soumia Alloui found people starting to line up in the blazing Sahara sun as early as eleven in the morning to get the Ramadan treats. By three in the afternoon, the hot and ravenous customers got so numerous that they caused traffic jams in the neighborhoods of the most famous zalabia shops. Whereas in the Middle East, zalabia are more or less the same thing as luqmat al-qadi, here, in Algeria, the batter is poured through a funnel to make long straight strips—a little like a rectilinear funnel cake. You really do need divine assistance to wait until sundown before biting into one—hot, crisp, and succulent with sweet syrup.

not made at home but rather bought from a specialist for religious festivals, especially the breaking of the fast at Ramadan.

Ramadan, the ninth month of the Islamic calendar, is supposed to be dedicated to fasting and spiritual regeneration. From sunup to sundown, an observant Muslim is expected to abstain from food and drink and meditate on religious matters. You'd think that people would lose weight during Ramadan, but it turns out that the opposite is true. Self-denial during daylight seems to give permission to many to overdo it at night.

Perhaps more fanatical about their Ramadan donuts than most, Algerians line up for hours before sundown for their *zalabia*, as

The shape and composition of the Ramadan sweets vary from place to place, but the craving for carbs and fat after a long day of fasting is common to most parts of the Muslim world. So much so that prices for oil, sugar, and honey spike during the monthlong fast. Shops jack up their prices too. People complain, but the higher prices seem to have no impact on their sweets intake—or take the air out of their ballooning waistlines.

The donut culture of the Muslim world extends far beyond the Middle East. To the West, many of Spain's fried treats have

*THE DONUT*

medieval Arabic precedents. In the east, Persians are just as obsessed with their version of *zulbia* (as it's called in Iran), which takes the form of a crisp spiral made with a batter of wheat starch and yogurt. India has a version of this as well. A thousand years ago, when Persian-speaking invaders rode into the subcontinent, they made sure to pack not only the Koran but also recipes for all sorts of delicious pastries. This is how Pakistanis and Indians learned to make the candy-like tangles of fried dough called *jalebi* (a corruption of the word *zulbia*). The Muslim invaders also brought a round fritter that eventually became gulab jamun. (*Gulab* comes from the Persian word for rosewater, while *jamun* refers to a local fruit of roughly this size.) In India, this juicy, sweet-scented morsel is about the size of a Ping-Pong ball. The recipe is more complex than in the Middle East, requiring a mixture of dried and fresh milk thickened with flour. But as in Iran, the mixture is fried and soaked in rosewater syrup.

Given how obsessed Indians are with sweets of every description, it's likely they already had plenty of fried treats before the foreign interlopers arrived. At least that's the impression you get from King Somesvara III, the sometime ruler of a middling medieval kingdom not far from today's Mumbai,

In South Asia, everyone knows you want to get your *gulab jamun* fresh and hot.

who wrote a sort of idiot's guide to kingship. Exhaustive and also at times delightfully kinky, the how-to manual gives the impression that the king had too much time on his hands. He gives advice on topics as varied as religion, interior design, and child rearing. He has opinions on the best sorts of umbrellas and the best kinds of beds—and

## SUFGANIYOT

Visit Israel during Hanukkah and you may be forgiven for thinking that the holiday is all about eating jelly donuts. You'll find them in a dozen flavors, the traditional ones filled with strawberry jam and butterscotch cream but also trendy new flavors such as crème brûlée, pistachio custard, tiramisu, halvah cream, and half a dozen variations on chocolate. Despite their present-day ubiquity, jelly donuts are a bit of an arriviste in the Holy Land, brought there by Jews from Eastern Europe, who had appropriated the habit of frying jelly donuts for the midwinter holiday from their German and Polish neighbors. *Sufganiyot* are nothing but *Krapfen*. Understandably the German name had to go, so Hebrew linguists came up with a term derived from an ancient word meaning "sponge." Apparently the holiday donuts' modern-day popularity dates from the 1920s when professional bakers made a big push to replace the homemade latkes (potato pancakes) popular among Eastern European Jews, with commercially produced donuts.

plenty of tips about what to do in those beds. His majesty also includes a selection of donut recipes.

As you'd expect of someone who advocates variety in sexual partners, the good king offers us an eclectic assortment of fried sweets. There's a sugar-sweetened donut (more like a donut hole) made with wheat flour and scented with cardamom and pepper, which is shaped into small balls and cooked in ghee. A similar, supercrispy treat is made with chickpea flour; another uses black lentil flour and gets dunked in sugar syrup, much like its Middle Eastern cousins. Perhaps the most intriguing is a recipe for a cheese-based fritter—mainly because most modern Indians would still recognize it. To make it, you form balls out of a dough of fresh cheese curds mixed with rice flour, fry these in ghee, and then soak them in cardamom-scented syrup. I imagine the king feeding the morsels—tender, buttery, and dripping with the perfumed syrup—to his favorite as she lies resplendent on a silk-lined bed.

Most of these fritters still exist and in more than one variation. Still, if Somesvara were alive today, I'd bet he'd

Jalebi are indispensable to many South Asian holidays.

go for something called a *ledikeni,* if only because it is named after a feisty—and almost royal—lady. The lady in question was Countess Charlotte Canning, the wife of the Indian viceroy Charles Canning. The tall, striking brunette arrived in India in 1856, more interested in roaming the hot and dusty roads of the British raj and painting watercolors than playing hostess back in her Calcutta palace. In between her official duties, she managed to produce scores of accomplished paintings. She also found time to send letters to her sometime mentor Queen Victoria about local conditions. There were, however, no pictures of sweetmeats and no word of fried dough balls in the missives to Buckingham Palace. If there had been, presumably the queen would not have been amused. When it came to Indian sweets, the English mostly seemed horrified by them. But they were awfully polite. Which was most likely Lady Canning's reaction when she got her present of syrup-soaked fritters.

According to the story, a prominent Indian functionary sent the sweets to Lady Canning, who graciously accepted them. Much like the medieval king's cheese fritters, ledikeni are made with fresh curd cheese and kneaded with a little flour, though here you get a bonus in the form of a filling of molten raw sugar—as you bite into one, the concealed reservoir spills its sweet juices. Whether she tasted the sweets or not is unknowable, but if she did, she might have found them to her liking—the caramelized spheres are reminiscent of the treacle tastes of a British raj nursery. Sadly, the talented aristocrat didn't have much time to explore the sweet or the bitter side of India. She succumbed to malaria some five years after she arrived. Whether it was her premature death or simply the association with the British rulers, the dessert, with its Anglicized name, became all the rage among Calcutta yuppies in the following decades.

While fried dough is associated with certain holidays in the Muslim and Jewish world, in Hinduism, the very act of frying sanctifies the food, as long as the fat in question is ghee. Every fluid (and yes I do mean *every* fluid) that a cow produces is sacred to some degree, but clarified butter, aka ghee, tops the list. According to one Hindu legend, the gods fished ambrosia, the nectar of immortality, out of a primordial ocean of roiling ghee. I take that to mean that the food of the gods is essentially a donut. Admittedly I have not yet found a swami to confirm my supposition. What is indisputable is that fried dough—in enough shapes and textures to exhaust even King Somesvara's appetites—is indispensable to many of India's religious observances and rituals.

Diwali, the eight-day party in honor of the goddess Lakshmi, and the closest thing Hinduism has to Christmas, is a time to eat fried sweets of every description, some based on rice, others on wheat, and yet others on legume flour. Most especially, there are *laddus*. These are made by deep-frying drops of bean- or wheat-flour-based batter, soaking these in syrup, and then squeezing them into a ball. As you bite into each droplet, it pops its sugary contents. Because of the way they are made, it used to be traditional to send laddus to children on their six-month birthday, since this is the age when babies first begin to open and close their fists. However, laddus are given on many other special days too.

In my case, the occasion occurred while waiting to be interviewed on Kolkata Television. When I arrived at the station, I was ushered into a crowded waiting room that had all the charm of an inner-city emergency room. As I was waiting for my moment in the Bengali spotlight, the doors opened to a vision worthy of Bollywood. A teen starlet, her sari trembling in the sputtering fumes of the air conditioner, fluttered into the room holding a tray of vibrant yellow laddus. I was expecting her to break into song, but instead she presented me with the fried treat and marked my forehead with vermilion bindi. I felt blessed, in more ways than one. And that, I discovered, was the whole point. The day was a holiday dedicated to brothers (and by extension male colleagues), and both the mark and the sweet were meant as a blessing. As I carefully nibbled my laddu, trying to avoid making a syrupy mess, it dawned on me that we might have Valentine's Day all wrong. Instead of men sending chocolates to their objects of affection, maybe their girlfriends should send boxes of donuts to their beaus.

## DONUT DEBAUCHERY

Sweets are associated with holiday feasts the world over, however we in the West seem to feel the need to bring guilt to the table as well. Whereas the Hindu deities are generally a sensual and fun-loving bunch, the God of the monotheistic religions is nothing if not a prude. After all, number one and two on the list of the seven deadly sins are gluttony and lust! Providentially, as every good Catholic knows, you have to sin before you can repent. By that logic, since Lent is the lengthiest and most profound period of repentance, it needs to be preceded by the deepest depravity. It's the same idea as Ramadan: you need the feast so you can tolerate the fast.

So we Catholics invented Carnival. And from Lisbon to Linz, from Valencia to Venice, in Europe, the pre-Lenten holiday is celebrated with fried pastry. But why donuts? The answer is simple: hog fat. Since Christians were supposed to abstain from meat products for the forty days of Lent, they had to figure out something to do with the lard that accumulated over the winter butchering season. And what better use for all that animal fat than frying up great platters of donuts? For ordinary people, donuts became associated with joyful excess, a real-life version of the mythical country of Cockaigne, where the houses had fences of bratwurst and the pine trees were hung with donuts instead of pinecones—as the sixteenth-century German poet Hans Sachs described the fairy-tale land. For the few days of Mardi Gras, at least, the rules of a peasant's miserable existence could be inverted, a spare diet of stale bread could be substituted with a blissful abundance of freshly fried donuts.

In Venice they've been at this since the Middle Ages. In Carnival's Renaissance heyday, men and women used to switch clothes, nuns took on less virtuous habits, and masked men murdered their enemies in plain sight. Sure, the authorities tried to put a stop to this, variously banning masks at night, outlawing cross-dressing, and restricting weapons, but a lot of good it did. What finally almost did kill the holiday was Napoleon's 1797 invasion and the Austrian occupation that followed his ouster. For some reason, the Austrian police couldn't abide armed, masked Venetians lurking in the city's abundant alleys. (The Austrians

In Venice, as elsewhere, the frying of donuts was often an outdoor affair. Specialized donut makers went where their customers were.

weren't a complete loss, they brought their jelly donuts—but more on that later.) Subsequently, Venetian Carnival traditions were on life support for almost two hundred years until the party was officially revived in 1979.

I visited some half dozen years after that and truth be told, my first glimpse of the resuscitated festival didn't exactly inspire confidence. When I tumbled off the train after a very long hour of sardine-like intimacy with my fellow revelers, the neighborhood near the station had all the vibe of a rock concert gone bad: groups of glassy-eyed teens slumped in church doorways, college-age kids projectile vomiting into the canals. I almost got on the next train out of there. Thankfully, as I moved away from the railway, the bad acid trip was gradually replaced by a happy, hallucinatory panorama of good fairies perched on arching bridges and medieval jesters cavorting on the embankments even as gondolas draped with ravishing drag queens and elegant Casanovas slipped through the canals. And then there were the donuts. Venice's traditional *frittelle di carnevale* are a yeast-raised, spiced, and booze-spiked donut fit to bursting with dried fruit and pine nuts. They are to American sinkers what Liberace is to Pat Boone. And those are what I like to call the more abstemious version. My carnival funk finally cleared only when I stumbled on a bakery that specialized in *frittelle* with zabaglione filling. These use the same choux dough as French nun's farts, but instead of being hollow, they are filled with a boozy, succulently creamy filling that oozes out with every bite. They would surely tempt even the most pious sister to gluttony and lust.

Venice has a tradition of fried dough as old as the pre-Lenten debauch. I'm particularly fond of a treat recorded in a cookbook around 1400 called *Fritelle da Imperadore magnifici* (magnificent fritters worthy of an emperor) made by stirring egg whites, flour, and pine nuts into ricotta. What made these airy pillows worthy of the name was a generous sprinkling of powdered sugar—a pricy luxury in those days. But does the tradition go back even further than that? Certainly the ancient world had fritters made of fresh cheese and others made of a dough not unlike the one used for nun's farts. It would be lovely to think that the techniques were preserved in hilltop monasteries even as the barbarians raged in the valleys below. Perhaps some future donut historian will be able to connect the dots between Cato's honey-dipped cheese puffs and the imperial ricotta-based morsels, or the other fried delights for that matter. For now, we can only speculate.

One popular Venetian donut that decidedly has no local ancestor is the *krapfen* (the Italians omit the Teutonic upper case) or custard-filled donut. One of the nice things about these fried pastries is that they are available year-round, unlike the city's Carnival fritters. To get the full krapfen experience, I like to visit Pasticceria Tonolo, a prim little temple to all things sweet some way off the main tourist drag. Around 10:00 AM or so is a good time since by this point many Venetians are in need of a pick-me-up. Men in studiously disheveled suits stop by to chat, flirt, and sip a little espresso. Ladies of a certain age gossip sotto voce over a macchiato and a krapfen—carefully sinking their teeth into the gently yielding dough so that the cream filling doesn't spurt onto their Prada scarves. You don't go to Tonolo just for the donuts; you go for the cream filling. Franco Tonolo tells me that traditionally it has always been the women of the family who have made the pastry cream. "My father made the pastry but my mother made the cream," he confides before going on to bemoan the state of the art in other pastry shops today. Many bakeries now buy their krapfen frozen and then simply fry them as needed. "It is so much more convenient for them," he grumbles. He makes, rolls, proofs, and fries the dough each and every morning before filling them with his wife's luscious cream. Come early, the donuts are gone by midday.

# DONUTS OF THE WORLD

Around the globe, there are dozens of ways that human genius has figured out to concoct fried dough treats. They are puffed up with yeast, baking powder, beaten eggs, or even beer. Wheat is most typical in the dough, but corn- and even legume-based flours can enter the mixture. Some are made with fresh curd cheese and others with yogurt, milk, or just plain water. They come in tangled strings, knotted strips, batons, disks, squares, and, of course, a multitude of rings. The following is hardly a comprehensive list, but it does give a taste of the possibilities.

In **France**, they're terrifically imprecise in their use of the word *beignet*. Sometimes it's a fruit fritter, other times a puffed morsel of choux paste—as in *pet de nonne*, also sometimes called *beignet soufflé*—while in many cases it comes closer to what we'd call a raised donut. What's more, the regional names defy categorization. In Lyons, *bugnes* are a sort of twisted raised pastry a little like a Pennsylvania *fastnacht*. Along the Atlantic coast, something similar is called a *merveille*. In Provence, orange blossom–scented *oreillettes* (little ears) resemble crisp crullers in consistency. The closest thing to a cake-style donut is an Alsatian baking powder–leavened fritter called a *beignet rapide* or *püpperchen* in the local dialect.

Across **Central Europe**, trying to make any sense of the fried dough tradition is an even more hopeless task than in France. One thing you will find throughout the region is the jelly donut (called by at least a half dozen names in the German-speaking regions), which can be filled with creamy fillings as well as fruit preserves. The terms Krapfen or *Faschinsgkrapfen* are typical of Austria and Bavaria, while *Pfannkuchen* is more common in Berlin and the north. Jelly donuts are not called *Berliner* in the capital, though they do carry this name in the western parts of the country. In Poland *paczki*, and in the Czech Republic *koblihy*, have traditionally been filled with prune butter or even sweetened farmer cheese. In the Rhineland they make the almond-shaped *Mutzenmandeln*, with almond meal added to the dough. From the same area, *Ballbäuschen* are fritters almost identical to Dutch *oliebollen*. *Knieküchle* (knee cakes) got their name because they have an indentation in the center, as if somebody poked their knee into the pastry. In parts of Switzerland they make *Fasnachtskiechli*, resembling a fried wafer. *Strauben*, or funnel cakes, are more common in the mountainous Austrian Tyrol.

In **Italy**, they've been frying dough for at least two thousand years, so it's hardly surprising that there are countless variations. Tuscany calls its filled donuts *bomboloni*, while in Veneto they're referred to by the German krapfen. Venice has any number of fritters, or *frittelle*, some made with yeast dough while others depend on choux pastry. *Galani* take the form of long, crispy, sugar-dusted ribbons. Elsewhere similar pastries are called *cenci* and *chiacchere*, just to name two. Naples is renowned for *zeppole*, which are traditionally made with an eggless flour-and-water dough that is fried in a ring. *Zeppole di San Giuseppe* use choux pastry and are filled with a lemony pastry cream once fried. *Struffoli* resemble Arab *zalabia*, though here they take the form of little droplets of fried dough that are subsequently bathed in honey syrup. Sicily is home to one of Italy's more obscure sweets, rectangular fried chickpea fritters called *pan-*

*elle dolci,* made for the feast of Santa Lucia.

Both **Portugal** and **Spain** have traditions that date back to the era of Muslim rule, if not earlier. In Spanish, the word *buñuelos* is about as meaningful as *beignet* in France (the two words are related). *Buñuelos de viento* are fried cream puffs served for All Saints' Day. Other sweet *buñuelos* use a yeast-leavened batter much like North African *zalabia.* In Mexico, *buñuelos Mexicanos* resemble a fried flour tortilla topped with raw sugar syrup. They are similar to *sopaipillas* and cousins to what Native Americans call fry bread. In Colombia, *buñuelos* are made with fresh cheese and cornstarch. *Rosquillas* (also *roscos*) are by definition donut-shaped, though the term can refer to both fried cookies and baked ring-shaped treats. There's a picture of these in a still life painted in 1627 by Juan van der Hamen y Leon that hangs in Washington's National Gallery. They're traditional to Easter. And throughout the Spanish-speaking world you find the extruded water-and-flour-paste fritters called *churros.* Portugal has its own vast dessert repertory that sometimes overlaps with its larger neighbor.

There are all sorts of fritters called *filhos*—some are ribbon-like fritters scented with orange, others are more donut-like. *Borrachões* are pastry rings flavored with brandy. In some regions, *sonhos* are the same as the Spanish *buñuelos de viento* (formerly they used to be dipped in sugar syrup though a sprinkling of sugar is now more common), elsewhere they are a yeast-raised donut and closely related to the *malassadas* of the Azores and Madeira. The recipe for this last fry cake made its way with Portuguese immigrants all the way to Hawaii where *malasadas* (sic) are now sometimes stuffed with tropical fillings such as guava or coconut. In Hawaii, Shrove Tuesday has come to be known as Malasada Day due to the imported Carnival donut tradition.

In **North Africa** and the **Middle East**, yeast-based fritters take the form of irregular rings (Morocco's *sfenj*), syrup-soaked donut holes (Egypt's *zalabia,* also *luqmat al qadi*), or funnel cakes (*zlabia* in Tunisia, *zulbia* in Iran). In Somalia *skaramati* (also *burka macaan*) are tangy with yogurt and aromatic from their bath in cardamom-scented syrup. Turkey's *tulumba* and Iran's *balmieh* are syrup-soaked cousins (or more likely aunts and uncles) to Spanish *churros.* North Africa is also home to a host of fried cookies such as Tunisia's conch-shell-shaped *debla* or Morocco's rosebud-shaped *chebbakia.*

**South Asia**'s *jalebi* are an obvious descendant of their Middle Eastern lookalikes. The violently colored, syrup-soaked tangles of dough are made extra crisp by the addition of gram (chickpea) flour. In Bengal they make a spiral-shaped fritter, *chanar jilepi,* out of a fresh curd cheese. *Pantua,* and the similar *ledikeni,* are also based on fresh curd cheese, though here the sweets are ball shaped. *Laddus* are made round by squeezing together fried droplets of a batter that can be made with wheat, semolina, chickpea or bean flour. All of these are soaked in syrup typically flavored with rosewater or cardamom. The closest thing you'll find to a western donut is probably a *gulab jamun,* which looks a lot like a donut hole, or the ring-shaped *balushahi,* which you could almost mistake for a donut.

Krapfen, as the name would indicate, are German and were introduced to the Venetians by the Austrian invaders following Napoleon's demise. The fry cakes share the same ancestor as the American jelly donut, the Bismarck, and the Boston cream. Though the proud inhabitants of the ancient port had little use for the arrogant foreign officers who lorded over the cafés on Piazza San Marco during Austria's sixty-year occupation, the Venetians just couldn't resist adding another fried dessert to their already rich donut larder. It probably helped that krapfen have no local holiday associations, which meant that you could eat them irrespective of season. That was less true in their Central European homeland, where they were still very much thought of as a holiday treat. Even today, in their Teutonic fatherland, donuts still mean Carnival.

## DONUTS, DONUTS ÜBER ALLES

Just across the Alps, in Austria's mountainous Tyrol, Carnival takes a rather different form from what you find in the stylish Italian metropolis. On the days leading up to Ash Wednesday, Alpine villagers don masks that would give the Brothers Grimm nightmares. In long-isolated mountain communities, the residents transform themselves into macabre witches, giant burly bears, and gruesome forest gnomes. In one locally beloved ritual, men and boys stuff their shirts with hay and stumble like hunchbacks around the town square while others try to flip the stuffed shirts, like turtles, onto their backs. In other villages, men, wearing women's dresses and masks, parade down Main Street, all the while whirling and snapping giant whips. It's all great fun—in a Germanic sort of way.

For those whose idea of fun doesn't include whips and cross-dressing, there are the *Faschingskrapfen* (Carnival donuts), great mountains of plump filled donuts, everywhere you look. The bakery windows are full of them, the train station has special donut stands set up for the occasion, even the mountaintop ski lodges feature displays of the season's pastries. There's nothing quite like sinking your teeth into the warm, doughy pillows in the icy alpine air. Should you get tired of the classic jam-filled variety, you can opt for custard, chocolate cream, or even the local answer to zabaglione, *Eiercognac*, a brandy-spiked eggnog custard.

Elsewhere in the German-speaking world, other sorts of fried dough come out for the midwinter celebration. In the region that abuts France, square donuts, often with a couple of slits cut into the center, are served with a thick dusting of sugar. In parts of Switzerland, they twist and form the dough into knots; elsewhere they use special presses to create a rose shape. Anybody but a linguist would be foolish to try to list all the names for these confections, but even among the pros success isn't guaranteed. The singularly obsessive, four-volume *Wortatlas der deutschen Umgangssprach* (*The Word Atlas of German Speech*) maps out twenty-two variations of yeast-raised donuts, yet that barely scratches the surface.

How old the tradition of frying dough is in this part of the world is anybody's guess. It's perfectly plausible that the idea was introduced by the Romans, who once had settlements in places like Vienna and Cologne. Certainly the region had plenty of lard and at least a modicum of wheat back then. The first documented mention of the donut in German comes from the early-thirteenth-century epic *Parzifal* by Wolfram von Eschenbach. The poem follows the eponymous knight of the Round Table as he traipses through a mythical land on a quest for the Holy Grail. There are the usual medieval chivalric shenanigans, but to donut scholars the only event that matters occurs in Book Four, when Parzifal arrives in a war-ravaged land ruled by the ill-fated Queen Conwiramurs. This country is so desolate, the narrator writes, that even mead was in short supply, and the locals were so deprived they had never heard the sound of frying Trühending Krapfen. (Trühending was a town renowned for its fry cakes.) Our hero, after seducing and marrying the queen, soon heads for the hills, presumably after the grail, though I wonder if it wasn't just an excuse to stop by Trühending to pick up a freshly fried dozen for the road.

The medieval donut mecca still exists. It is now called Wassertrüdingen and should you walk into a bakery and ask for Krapfen, what you'll get is a jelly donut. The local chamber of commerce makes a big deal of the very oblique *Parzifal* connection, but despite the enthusiasm of local historians, we actually have no idea what those early medieval fried treats looked or tasted like. One thing that's dead certain is that they weren't jelly donuts. The fourteenth-century cookbook *Das Buch von guter Speise* gives you four filling options, all of which involve spiced apples. These are combined with nuts, honey, grapes, or—that perennial favorite—pike guts. What the book's author doesn't tell you is how to make the outside pastry. It might have been a yeast dough, but maybe not. A hundred years later, a similar recipe in the best-selling Bavarian cookbook, *Küchenmeisterei,* for "*gefüllete Krapffen*" (filled donuts), does specify a yeast dough but other sources suggest pastry dough. (Incidentally, here you have the option of using pears, apples, calf brains, or game bird hash for the filling.) It's perfectly plausible that *Parzifal*'s donuts were actually turnovers or even something resembling fried ravioli and, like Italian stuffed pasta, were unlikely to have been sweet; as late as the nineteenth century, spinach- and fish-filled donuts weren't considered weird.

In some cases there was no filling at all. Peasants, who couldn't afford sugar but wanted a sweet donut treat, might dip plain, raised lumps of fried dough in plum or pear butter or a kind of honey-sweetened soup. Sugar was extravagantly expensive, and consequently so were the jams and jellies that we now take for granted. In the Hapsburg Empire, which dominated the Germanic donut ecosystem, these fruit-and-sugar mixtures were the exclusive preserve of the guild of confectioners. If you wanted to buy jam for your Krapfen, there was no alternative. Accordingly the jam-filled variety cost easily double the price of the plain kind. During the Napoleonic Wars (admittedly a time when sugar was extra pricy), unfilled donuts cost two to three *Kreuzer* (a silver coin), the filled variety four to eight, and the very finest kind as much as twelve. To give a sense of what that meant, the best jelly donut was the price of a good multi-course dinner!

The Viennese didn't seem to care about the exorbitant price, or at least it didn't stop their Krapfen cravings. Their obsession went back to the days when the city was still a two-horse town. There were professional donut bakers (who seemed to have been all women) at least as far back as 1486. We know this because that year they were specifically enjoined from frying fish by city authorities overseeing the commonweal. Unlike in Germany, fish gut-flavored donuts would not be tolerated in Vienna.

The donut frenzy peaked in the baroque period, perhaps because by now the cost of sugar had dropped sufficiently so that jam was widely available, even if it continued to be pricy. For *Fasching*, as Carnival is called here, the city's paper of record was full of ads from shops advertising their *Faschingskrapfen*. The editors even ran occasional donut shop reviews. The imperial court got into the action too. During the holiday they organized contests in donut marksmanship. This was a little like skeet shooting but with fried dough balls shot into the sky instead of clay pigeons. Apparently the best shot could win a set of silver pistols. The donut mania hit its zenith in 1815 as all of Europe looked to Vienna to sew Europe back together after Napoleon's megalomaniacal wars had torn it to shreds. At that year's Congress of Vienna, the city played host to the whole continent's powerbrokers. There were two emperors and empresses, four kings, one queen, two crown princes, three princesses, and a pair of grand duchesses accompanied by battalions of hangers-on and great armies of servants and cooks. The full quantity of everything they ate has not been recorded, but according to press accounts, they consumed at least eight to ten million donuts during the 1815 Carnival season alone!

To the Viennese, donuts weren't just donuts. A decade after the 1815 Congress, F. G. Zenker, a cookbook author and some-time chef to princes, pointed out that by that point, Krapfen had become a national dish. Those were the days, though, when the jam-filled treats were still special, whereas in Vienna today they're as ubiquitous and common as Dunkin' Donuts are in America. Google "Austria's national dish" and Krapfen don't even register. The papers don't bother with seasonal donut shop reviews, and Carnival season passes without a single fried-pastry shooting contest. Nowadays, most Austrians will undoubtedly point to the Sacher torte as the national dessert. The cake may be delicious and sophisticated, but how much fun is it? And what challenge would there be in shooting down a flying Sacher torte?

Just about every café in Vienna has airy jelly donuts—no longer a seasonal treat—on the menu year round.

## TILTING AT DONUTS

Spaniards, like Italians and Germans, consider Carnival donuts part of their Catholic birthright even though here, ironically, fried dough most likely predates Christianity and perhaps even hog fat itself.

There are certainly old Spanish sweet-meats that sound a lot like they originated in Ancient Rome. A sixteenth-century Catalan recipe for Xativa "oranges" describes fried, honey-dipped cheese balls that seem not so different from Cato's fried cheese morsels. Other kinds of fried dough appear to

## GUTTER DONUTS

Given the cultural significance of the donut in the lands of the old Hapsburg Empire, it's hardly surprising that the word would end up in the region's slang. And the result isn't always pretty. In the nineteenth century, when buxomness was more fully appreciated, a young woman might sometimes hear that she was as pretty as a Krapfen. In Czech, a damsel described as donut-like used to mean that she was adorable in a voluptuous sort of way. Alas, the Hapsburg Empire isn't what it used to be. In contemporary Austrian usage, if you call a girl a Krapfen, it's an insult, and a *Krapfengesicht* ("donut face") is not considered an attractive sight at all. Krapfen is also slang for an accident. Worse, an *Arschenkrapfen* is a compound word made up of "arse" and "donut," which I would prefer not to translate here, but suffice it to say that it bears some relationship to the Czech *kravské koblihy*, literally "cow donuts," or what we'd call cow pies.

date back to the days of Muslim rule. One donut-rich collection of Andalusian recipes from the thirteenth century includes clear directions on how to make *zulabiyya* (as it was then spelled). Here it was a funnel cake made by drizzling a thin stream of batter through a hole to create a knotted tangle of dough. (Three hundred years later, the Catalan cookbook calls these *rosquillas*.) Another medieval Muslim-era cookbook gives instructions for spiced, honey-dipped braided donuts and ring-shaped fried cookies too. It also explains how to make something called "stuffed *isfunj*," which sounds absolutely scrumptious—like a happy coupling of baklava and a donut. It's a ball-shaped donut made with leavened wheat dough, filled with a honey-sweetened filling of ground almonds, walnuts, and pistachios. There was also a plain-Jane, unstuffed variety that you still find today in Morocco under the name of *sfenj*. There, today's cooks are more likely to form the sticky yeast dough into a rough ring instead of a ball before frying, giving it the appearance of a ragged American sinker with a crisp, lightly chewy texture that's irresistible.

One thing our cookbooks don't tell us is if these early Andalusian donuts were made for Ramadan as they are today, but there's no reason to think they weren't. Certainly the Jews of Spain served something similar for Hanukkah. Like their Muslim neighbors, they fried the fritters in oil, which in later years drew the suspicion of the Holy Inquisition. After Isabella forced Jews to convert or be expelled in 1492, one of the most common ways the church authorities caught suspected, secretly observant Jews was to spy on their eating habits. Frying in olive oil instead of lard was sure to arouse suspicion—or worse. Many Inquisition trials depended on the testimony of kitchen snitches. Yet despite their antagonism, the Christians absorbed more than one habit from the Muslims and Jews they ejected. Fried dough became a favorite snack even if lard replaced the oil of the expelled.

The very first donut fest described in a novel takes place in Spain, in Cervantes's *Don Quixote,* written around 1610. In this tragicomic tale of chivalry gone awry, the leading players couldn't be more different: the eponymous knight dreams of a world full of damsels in distress even while his trusty sidekick, Sancho Panza, has his sights on more immediate pleasures. During one lull between jousting at windmills, Don Quixote is invited to a wedding, launching Sancho into a state of salivating suspense. Arriving at the feast, he is not disappointed. A whole meadow has been commandeered by the wedding party's chefs, who are preparing enough food to feed an army. A great bullock stuffed full of suckling pigs roasts upon a spit; stewpots big enough to swallow a sheep simmer on low fires, and tall piles of game are readied for the grill. There are two dozen skins full of wine and stacks of cheese and bread. And donuts: "Two caldrons of oil, larger than a dyer's vat, stood ready for frying dough balls; and, with a couple of stout peels, they took them out when fried, and dipped them in another kettle of prepared honey, that stood by." Poor Sancho, he never gets to taste them. No sooner does he begin his feast with three pullets and a couple of geese than he's snagged from a stewpot when the bride runs off with a former suitor. Romantic that he is, Don Quixote follows the love-besotted couple, and despondent Sancho is bereft of both wine and donuts. That's what you get for following dreamers.

It's a pity that Cervantes didn't give us a recipe, but at least we do know that the donuts Sancho Panza never got to taste were dipped in honey, which makes them sound remarkably similar to their Arabic predecessor. However, one intriguing thought is that Sancho's honey-dipped fritters were altogether something else. Maybe, just maybe, they were those Spanish farts cited in medieval French sources. In Cervantes's day, these were called *buñuelos de viento* (wind fritters) a name they still retain. In contemporary Spain, they are a traditional treat for All Saints' Day.

These windy fritters were typically ball shaped, but there were others that used a similar dough to make churros, or "*fruta de xeringa*" (syringe fritters) as they were known at the time.

In Spain and other parts of the Spanish-speaking world, churros are a natural match for hot chocolate.

The process hasn't changed much since then. Churros are still made by extruding a cooked water-and-flour dough through a star-shaped die or piping tip into hot fat. You find the long, crispy, sugar-and-cinnamon-dusted fritters just about anywhere Spanish is spoken.

In Cervantes's day, they used to be even more ubiquitous. The German cookbook author Sabrina Welserin calls them *Strauben* in her 1553 cookbook. (In Germany today *Strauben* are more like American funnel cakes.) Seventeenth-century English manuals give instructions "To fry Paste out of a Syringe or Butter-squirt." The French had something similar, as did the Italians. Churros aren't so different from Neapolitan zeppole. In the hometown of pizza and Sophia Loren, they make the fritters with the same sort of hot-water-and-flour dough used in Mexico for churros, but instead of ribbons, they form it into circles much like a donut. How far back this ring-shaped fritter goes is hard to know; certainly Italians have been making bagel-shaped baked sweet breads since at least the Renaissance. Could the fried donut-shaped zeppole be as old as that?

Whether these treats were sacred or secular, square, round or circular, filled with jam or soaked in syrup, the Old World was a garden of fried delights. The trouble was, it only bloomed on special occasions. But that would change as Europeans put down roots on the other side of the Atlantic. In the New World, fast seldom followed the feast. The fences really were made of bratwurst, and tree branches groaned under the weight of donuts. Or so it seemed to many immigrants. Common laborers could eat meat seven days a week, and special-occasion foods like donuts were an everyday indulgence for everyone. In the United States especially, donuts came to represent the mythical country of plenty, a glazed, fat-rich, ring-shaped symbol of the promised land.

# 2

# AMERICA THE BOUNTIFUL

*DONUT FEAST*

In May 1861, the Third Regiment Maine Volunteer Infantry set up some eighty canvas tents on the broad lawn in front of Augusta's state capitol to get ready for the influx of recruits arriving to join the Union army. In a scene that was repeated across the North and the South, Maine's teenaged boys and young men walked or hitched a ride to the capital. Some, I expect, signed up out of a sense of duty; but others were probably just bored with life on the farm, and I bet many joined to snag the $100 they'd get as a bonus on enlistment. In Maine, some towns offered an additional bonus of $200. For a seventeen-year-old farm boy, the chance to collect the equivalent of six years' wages must have seemed like a good deal—at least at the time.

As the mud-caked farmhands and salt-crusted fishermen trickled in, they were handed brand-new uniforms, overcoats, even pajama bottoms! They spent four weeks drilling, learning to use their bayonet-tipped muskets, and marching around as if it were the Fourth of July. It all promised to be a grand adventure, and the boys in blue were the toast of the town. In the last full week of training, the ladies of Augusta decided to throw the recruits a party, and since this was New England, the occasion would naturally be celebrated with donuts. Piles and piles of donuts. Donuts in so many varieties that it would turn a pink-and-orange Dunkin' Donuts green with envy. "The cooks and housewives of the city had for days been elaborating the viscous compound," one writer later reported on the vats of dough that had to be prepared. The event was so notable that newspapers as far south as Baltimore picked up the story of the "Feast of Doughnuts." The following report ran in the *Baltimore Sun* on June 29, nearly a month after the actual event.

> The ladies of Augusta, Me., one day last week, distributed over fifty bushels of doughnuts to the Third Volunteer regiment of Maine. A procession of the ladies, headed by music, passed between double lines of troops, who presented arms, and were afterward drawn up in hollow square [a military formation] to receive the welcome *dough*nation.
>
> Never before was seen such an aggregate of doughnuts since the world began. The circumambient air was redolent of doughnuts.—Every breeze sighed doughnuts—everybody talked of doughnuts. The display of doughnuts beggared description. There was the molasses doughnut and the sugar doughnut—the long doughnut and the short doughnut—the round doughnut and the square doughnut—the rectangular doughnut and the triangular doughnut—the single twisted doughnut and the double twisted doughnut—the "light riz" [risen?] doughnut and the hard-kneaded doughnut—the straight solid doughnut and the circular doughnut, with a hole in the centre. There were doughnuts of all imaginary kinds, qualities, shapes, and dimensions. It was emphatically a feast of doughnuts, if not a flow of soul.

For the boys, this donut debauch would prove a short-lived prelude to the bloody years that awaited them. On June 5, the recruits of the Third Regiment filed onto the train bound for Washington. One in five wouldn't make it back.

## YANKEE CAKES

The reason that the *Baltimore Sun*'s readers were intrigued with the donut feast story was that it gave them a glimpse into the exotic and foreign ways of those quaint folk from Maine. Sure Marylanders knew what a donut was, but in their minds these sorts of fry cakes were Yankee food. Donuts had been a northeastern regional specialty ever since the founding of the

Republic—and probably well before that. Across the pond the English found the culinary habits of their rebellious cousins even more exotic. In 1825, the editors of London's *Literary Gazette*—undoubtedly astonished that Americans could even put pen to paper—ran an excerpt from Portland, Maine, native John Neals's recently published *Brother Johnson: or the New Englanders*. The *Gazette*'s editors couldn't help but note that "unlike other nations [America] had not worked up her way gradually from barbarism to civilization; she had no religion, no manners, and above all, no language, essentially her own." Notwithstanding, the publication was so taken with the author's description of the savages' primitive rites that it quoted in full Neals's description of a gut-bursting New England supper. This included several kinds of meat, vegetables, puddings and pies, and, of course, "dough nuts."

"In America," Neal writes, "puddings and pies, vegetables and meat, were all on the table at once…here were turnips, and potatoes; here were dough nuts, a kind of sweet cake fried in lard; honey comb, new butter, cheese, rye and Indian bread." Since many Englishmen would have never heard the term, the American author thought it

THE LADIES OF AUGUSTA TREATING THE THIRD MAINE TO DOUGHNUTS.

The story of the Feast of the Doughnuts was featured in newspapers throughout Union territory.

necessary to explain the exotic pastry to his European readers.

Fried dough makes a regular appearance in Yankee works of fact and fiction alike. Reporting on the manners and habits of Revolutionary-era New Englanders, *The Monthly Traveller* (a compilation of press reports) recalled, "on Sabbath day morning they generally had chocolate, coffee, or bohea tea…with it they had pancakes, doughnuts, brown toast, some sort of pie." In a memoir of farm life during George Washington's presidency, Sarah Smith Emery reminisces about donuts for Thanksgiving, donuts sent on sledding trips, donuts for snacks, even donuts sent out to the field during haying season. Sarah grew up in the heart of New England in Newburyport, Massachusetts, a stone's throw from New Hampshire. If you scour newspapers from the Republic's early years, you'll find donuts in the *Times of Boston*, in the *Berkshire Reporter*, and in the *Nantucket Evening Post,* yet oddly, east of the Hudson, America's periodicals give the impression of a donut desert.

Later, Civil War records show that New Englanders didn't just live off the memory of the donut feast back home, they even managed to fry them up deep in the heart of Dixie. In the spring of 1863, the volunteers of the Fifteenth Regiment, New Hampshire, were encamped near New Orleans and had raided the countryside for blackberries. And what does a Yankee do with blackberries? Make sauce for donuts, naturally—which is exactly what the mess dished up for supper that night. If letters back home can be believed, the boys from New Hampshire ate the fried pastries on a regular basis.

Southerners knew full well that donuts were Yankee food. Mary Randolph, a Virginia innkeeper and author of the first Southern cookbook, called them "Yankee Cakes." As late as 1918, people still recognized the connection. A World War I reporter filing a story for the *Cleveland Advocate* about conditions on the Western Front noted, "Every fighter over here might have been born in New England, where they eat 'em for breakfast, so pronounced is the reverence for the great American doughnut."

Needless to say, our informant from Cleveland didn't know the half of it. New Englanders, being of a practical bent, knew that donuts were appropriate for any time of day and for any meal. Breakfast was just the beginning. The Massachusetts-born philosopher, naturalist, tax evader, and, apparently, donut fancier Henry David Thoreau records having being offered a donut-rich New England breakfast during an 1855 excursion to Cape Cod. Having lodged in Wellfleet with a nonagenarian oysterman who regaled the visitors into the night with stories of his pre-Revolutionary youth, the transcendentalist author and his companion awoke the next day to a breakfast of "eels, buttermilk cake, cold bread, green beans, doughnuts, and tea." As breakfast baked and sizzled in the wide kitchen hearth, the oysterman resumed his monologue, all the while using the same fireplace as a spittoon to deposit his tobacco-laced saliva. Thoreau, who took careful note where the spittle landed, deemed it safe to limit himself to the donuts and some applesauce. My guess is that these were the nut-round, yeast-raised variety, crisp and puffy with a sweet, earthy note of molasses. No matter the recipe, the donuts must have been good, because, before hitting the road, the sage of Walden Pond and his companion filled their pockets with the deep-fried snacks. Donuts did seem to play the role of granola bars in their day. Many intrepid travelers were sent on their way with donuts and, often, cheese—no weirder a combination in its day than cheese with apple pie.

Of course, Yankee philosophers weren't the only New Englanders who had a thing for fry cakes for breakfast. In the spring of 1886, the *New York Times* reported on the execution of Allen Adams, an unrepentant murderer, in Northampton, Massachusetts. Before mounting the gallows, the foul-mouthed prisoner sat down to a morning meal of meat pie, crackers, tea, and donuts. Cursing his captors, he demanded eggnog as well, but he had to make do with the fried dough.

But let's face it: most New Englanders didn't much care when they ate their donuts. In 1844, housekeeping authority Mrs. Esther Allen Howland suggests a post-church lunch (she calls it dinner) of bread and butter, cheese, pie, and donuts in her *New England Economical Housekeeper*. She must have been especially fond of the cake variety, given that she includes five recipes. My favorite is a rich and buttery version that's almost like a deep-fried pound cake. Donuts for supper seemed to

## MIRACLES AND WONDERS

In pursuit of donuts and crullers in nineteenth-century cookbooks, I discovered volumes full of miracles and wonders. No, really, donuts called miracles and wonders. I was perplexed until I discovered that in Atlantic France, they make something called a *merveille*, which sometimes looks like a New Orleans beignet and other times a cookie-like cruller. So what's the connection? Most likely it's the Channel Island of Jersey where they still make—according to the BBC—something they call "Jersey Wonders or Mèrvelles." To make them, you cut a slit in a rectangle of dough, then twist the top end (of the oblong) through the hole. Whether the wonders got to America directly from France, French Canada, or the Channel Islands is the sort of mystery that defies solution. It's worth noting, though, that Thoreau's paternal grandfather hailed from Jersey. Could it be that the transcendentalist poet's weakness for fried dough ran in his blood?

have been common enough as well. Connecticut novelist Harriet Beecher Stowe reports on an evening meal of baked beans and donuts in her fictional depiction of New England life. An 1843 report from the New Hampshire Asylum for the Insane makes for less entertaining reading, but it too lists donuts as part of a supper menu that also included bread and butter, cheese, tea, and milk.

If we can believe Charles Wyllys Elliott's description of Puritan foodways, there was more to some of these donut suppers than just a surfeit of calories. According to the author of *New England History*, the Puritan harvest was little more than a prelude to Sodom. "At the supper table," the historian writes of the young settlers, "many a sweet thing was whispered behind a *dough-nut,* and many a sentiment tucked in a pie." Soon after, this would be followed by "singular sounds made in the shadow of all those Puritan 'stoops.'" It's well documented that New England did have an exceptionally high birthrate. Could it have been the donuts?

As a rule, the Puritans didn't go in much for fun of any sort. Certainly donuts weren't associated with pleasure-filled holidays as they were in Europe. The settlers of Plymouth Rock tolerated no Saints' Day processions, no Christmas festivals, and certainly no cross-dressing for Carnival. Eating and drinking were allowed—just as long as you didn't enjoy them too much—but heaven forfend that a raucous feast should have anything to do with religion. The result of this was that special-occasion foods, like donuts, lost their holiday associations. Instead, they became an everyday treat, to be munched on morning, noon, and night.

Wherever New Englanders went, donuts were sure to follow. Yankee sailors even insisted on them on the high seas. Annie Eliza Dow, the wife of the Maine-born captain Jonathan Dow, reports whipping up batches of cookies, donuts, a lemon pie, and a couple of cakes while anchored in Naples harbor in 1866. (Yankee captains often took their wives and children on long trading voyages.) Skeptical that Italy could offer anything edible, Mrs. Dow packed a roast chicken and donuts for a hike up Vesuvius later in their stay. Another captain's wife, Mary Lawrence, recalled being a guest on the whaler *Julian* off the coast of Alaska in 1857. It was quite the spread: the visitors were treated to a Sunday supper of oysters, cold duck, biscuits, preserved pears, mince pie, donuts, and cookies.

Frying donuts on board a whaling ship wasn't much of a stretch given the continuous supply of fresh whale oil. Betsey Stockton, an African American missionary who had hitched a ride on a whaler to Hawaii recalled a fresh whale kill in the South Atlantic in 1822: "The weather delightful; and the crew all engaged in making oil of two black fish [whales] killed yesterday. This is fine amusement for the missionaries. We have had corn parched in the oil; and doughnuts fried in it. Some of the company liked it very much. I could not prevail on myself to eat it." She was obviously in the minority.

There was a tradition that for every thousand barrels filled with oil, the crew would celebrate by firing up a kettle of whale grease and frying dough balls. You couldn't have asked for a better setup. The whaling ships were outfitted with giant cauldrons used to render the oil with skimmers handy for the task of scooping out donuts. As Ms. Stockton suggests, these sinkers must have tasted pretty fishy, but for sailors used to being up to their ears in whale guts, a little "eau de poisson" would have been hardly noticeable.

In 1845, Mary Brewster described the eagerness of her ship's crew as the donut orgy grew nearer: "At 7 PM boats got fast to a whale and at 9 got him to the ship. Men all singing and bawling Doughnuts. Doughnuts tomorrow as this will certainly make us 1,000 barrels." On the following day the fry fest was in full swing: "This afternoon the men are frying doughnuts in the try pots," she writes, "and seem to be enjoying themselves merrily."

## ORIGINS

So where did New Englanders pick up their fried dough obsession, or more to the point, where did they get the recipe, or recipes, for their daily donut feasts? One thing we know for sure is that by 1776, the thirteen states had at least three distinct fry cake cultures. In Pennsylvania, the German immigrants set up their pots of lard much as they had back home. In New York's Hudson Valley, Dutch Americans had their own particular old world tradition; then there were the eastern states, populated by predominantly English settlers with their donuts. Did the Puritans also bring their recipe from the old country?

Certainly fritters and frying were common in every part of Europe from at least the Middle Ages. A recipe from as early as 1430 gives instruction on how to make something called "cryspes" made by drizzling a pancake-like batter off the ends of your fingers into fresh grease. Curiously, it sounds a lot like earlier Arabic recipes. In eighteenth-century England, just as on the continent, Shrove Tuesday was celebrated with fritters or pancakes. Colonial-era English cookbooks are littered with fritters of every description. Some were fluffed up with beaten eggs; others were made with little more than beer, eggs, and flour. There were even occasional recipes that used yeast in much the same way early New England donut recipes did. But would any of these British dough balls pass muster at a Krispy Kreme or Tim Hortons? Well, maybe.

Early nineteenth-century print sources speak of something called a "donnut" or "dough-nut" in Baldock, a prominent market town in the English county of Hertfordshire. "Shrove Tuesday is long counted of by the 'juveniles,' by whom it is known as 'Dough-nut Day,'" a local correspondent jotted down in 1832, "it being usual for the 'mothers' to make good store of small cakes fried in hog's lard, placed over the fire in a brass kettle or skillet, called 'dough-nuts,' wherewith the 'younger fry' are plenteously regaled. Of their wholesomeness I cannot aver, but they are allowed to take precedence of pancakes and fritters." Could the tradition or at least the fry cakes have migrated here from Hertfordshire? Certainly a good number of the early Puritan settlers came from there. Hartford, Connecticut, is only the most prominent of several New England locales named after towns in the English county.

Curious about the connection, I picked up the phone and spoke to Brendan King, the chairman of the Baldock Museum and Local History Society. Did he know of any information that could shed light on the matter. No? Then could he possibly inquire? Mr. King promised to put a notice in the local history newsletter, a technique that reminded me more of the modus operandi of Sherlock Holmes than the modern donut e-scholar. Convinced that the trail was lost and that the origin of the New England donut would be consigned to obscurity, I moved on.

I should have had more faith in the methods of the fictional Baker Street detective. Some months later, I received a note from Dr. Heather Falvey of Cambridge University, who was in the final stages of editing a collection of recipes compiled by Baroness Elizabeth Dimsdale around 1800. Given that the baroness was born in 1732 and worked as a housekeeper before her rather late marriage in 1779, it's likely she collected the recipes in the second half of the century. And yes, one of the recipes is for something called "Dow Nuts." They are sweet, yeast-raised cakes, rolled and cut into "nuts" (that is, small cakes) with a jagging iron or pastry wheel. Except for being a little eggier, the recipe is virtually identical in both proportions and technique to recipes published some two generations later in the United States. Consequently, the conclusion that the American donut originates in England—my dear Watson—is elementary.

Of course New England's settlers didn't live in isolation. To the east, there were the beignet-mad neighbors in French Canada, and to the west the dough-ball-frying Dutch in New York. Even closer to home, there were the Germans. These economic and religious refugees arrived in the 1700s, mainly from southwestern Germany. Some settled in Maine, others in northwestern Massachusetts, and others stayed on in the Boston area. Each group must have had some influence on their English-speaking neighbors, eventually transforming the British fritter into that expansive list of varieties found at Augusta's Civil War donut feast.

## DONUT MELTING POT

Certainly every dough-frying immigrant group that settled in the New World brought its own version of the donut. Some even believe that Native Americans' fry bread can be seen as a sort of proto donut,

## A TASTE OF FREEDOM

When I visited Ellis Island some years back, I was struck by a quote on one of the panels in the former receiving station where so many future Americans arrived. It was from a Swedish immigrant who got her first taste of the promised land here. "When I arrived at Ellis Island," she remembered, "they served us coffee and donuts. This was the first time that I saw or ate a donut and I thought it was great! It tasted so good. Of course at home we didn't have anything like that." She was just one of many. For decades, volunteers from the YMCA, the Red Cross, the Salvation Army, and other organizations sweetened the immigration process by serving coffee and donuts to new arrivals. To hundreds of thousands of Europe's homeless, tempest-tossed refugees, a sip of coffee and a donut was their first taste of freedom.

though that's probably stretching the definition to the breaking point. More than likely, the first fritters arrived in what is now the United States with the Spanish, when they landed in today's Florida and New Mexico in the late 1500s. They had hogs and they had flour, so—though we have no record of it—it's easy enough to imagine them celebrating their first American Carnival season by frying up a batch of *buñuelos* just like they did back home.

The Dutch were probably at it pretty early too. There are fried pastries called *olie-koecken* in *De Verstandige Kock* (*The Sensible Cook*), a popular seventeenth-century Dutch cookbook. The recipe for these "oil-cakes" produced crisp and doughy raisin fritters, chock full of dried fruit, almonds, and apple, that were almost gingerbread-spicy with cinnamon, ginger, and cloves. We know that at least one of New York's wealthy Van Cortlands acquired a copy of a 1684 edition that included the crispy treat, though just when they got it or whether they even used it is unknowable. It seems likely, though, that at least some settlers held on to the Dutch tradition throughout the colonial period because recipes for "oly koeks" or "oly cooks" show up in more than one Dutch-American manuscript of the early years of the Republic. Some are made in the raisin-rich seventeenth-century style, while others use plain dough, like the fried treats of their German and New England neighbors.

Oddly, according to some sources, the close-knit Dutch-American communities seem to have kept their oil cakes mostly to themselves. If we are to believe a 1791 letter to New York's *Daily Advertiser,* they weren't much known on this side of the pond. The author, writing under the suggestive pseudonym Dough Nuts, describes a habit supposedly much in vogue among public officials back in Holland. "These worthy magistrates," writes our informant, "had long been in the practice of using 'Oeley Koechen, en Tee,' at all their public festivals." The combination was considered especially useful for clearing mental cobwebs. "Whenever their minds, from the profundity of their investigations, were in some degree beclouded, the 'Oeley Koechen, en Tee' were used, as the only antidotes to this grievous malady." Dr. Dough Nuts (as I like to think of him) finishes his note with the prescription that we too should adopt this salutary foreign regimen.

Washington Irving makes much the same point in his satirical *History of New York*. In the book, first published in 1809, the twenty-six-year-old son of British immigrants (writing under the nom de plume Diedrich Knickerbocker) describes a typical Dutch-American tea table as he (or rather his fictitious Dutch-American alter ego) imagined it might have been some two centuries earlier. He portrays it as groaning with "an enormous dish of balls of sweetened dough, fried in hog's fat, and called doughnuts, or olykoeks—a delicious kind of cake," adding, "at present scarce seen in this city, except in genuine Dutch families."

Really? It seems peculiar that New England was chockablock with donuts at this time but English New Yorkers hadn't picked up on their Dutch neighbors' delicious dough lumps. And it's especially odd given that we know of at least one Dutch donut baker who hawked her wares in downtown Manhattan. A visitor to the Oswego market (near today's Maiden Lane) recalled, "I think it was in 1796 that Mrs. Jeroleman set a table in the market to sell hot coffee for three-pence a cup, and dough-nuts for one penny each. Her table was the first of this description that I remember to have seen." It's impossible to know if she was selling the Dutch variety or catering to Anglo tastes with the kind of donut popular in New England. But whatever the form of her dough balls, she got stuck with an American moniker. Apparently, at 225 pounds, the baker bore a passing resemblance to her stock in trade. "As she moved in the market with her broad Dutch face," our reporter reminisced, "the butcher-boys sung out, 'there goes the large dough-nut.'"

But be careful how much of Irving's story you believe. In his day, Irving's *History of New York* was the equivalent of today's

The Dutch have been frying up chewy raisin-and-apple-filled *oliebollen* for centuries.

satirical news source, *The Onion*. It may well be that oly koeks were obscure in Irving's Manhattan circle of literary satirists, or simply that this was meant to be the opinion of the book's fabricated author. But a good story is hard to put down. Certainly Irving would be tickled pink that his great hoax still has the ring of truth.

## BETTER SAFE THAN SORRY

There are any number of terrible things that might happen in the absence of *fastnachts* for Mardi Gras, and the Pennsylvania Dutch, being a sensible race, don't go in for taking chances. According to one elderly source who was interviewed in the 1950s, anyone who doesn't eat *fastnachts* on Shrove Tuesday was sure to suffer from boils. Chickens wouldn't hatch, cabbages would shrivel, and the flax crop would fail if a family neglected the donut custom. There was also a danger of lice and rat infestation. On the other hand, for those who hewed true to ancestral tradition, there were all sorts of advantages. For example the lard that had been used for frying the pastries was extraordinarily effective in curing sores. When used to grease wagon wheels or spread on garden spades, it worked as a pest repellent.

By the 1800s, the Dutch treat did finally enter the American mainstream though as little more than a variation on a donut. Whereas real oly koeks were made with a relatively light dough that needed to be scooped and dropped into hot fat, Eliza Leslie, the Martha Stewart of antebellum America, suggests that you can transform regular donuts into "New York Oley Koeks" simply by tossing a handful of raisins and currants into the dough before rolling and cutting them.

While early American donuts may bear a passing family resemblance to Dutch oly koeks, early "dough nuts" are at times almost impossible to tell apart from the German fry cakes of Pennsylvania. The Pennsylvania Dutch (as the German immigrants were misnamed) mostly hailed from the western parts of what is now Germany, where they had a tradition of making donuts they called *Fastnachtkuchen*. (*Fastnacht*, literally "fast night," is German for Shrove Tuesday.) In America, this would get shortened to *fastnachts*, or even *fasnachts*. These have traditionally been made in the shape of squares or diamonds. Friederike Löffler, an eighteenth-century German cookbook author popular on both sides of the Atlantic, suggested long ago that you use a pastry wheel to make the job easier. Today, the Pennsylvania Dutch typically slash their rectilinear donuts in the center and pull them apart so there's a hole, a technique that you still find in the old country too. That said, saying anything definitive about the recipe used for today's *fastnachts* is asking for trouble. Some are made with a potato-based dough, while others use baking powder instead of yeast, some are square, others knotted, and you'll even encounter ones shaped like donuts. Many old-timers swear that the correct way of eating the fried pastry is to split it in half, slather it with molasses, and devour it as you would a bagel with cream cheese. In western Pennsylvania, locals would dunk this sweet molasses sandwich into saffron tea, though elsewhere other beverages were equally acceptable. For anyone who can't get their fill, each year in Columbia, Pennsylvania, Holy Trinity Catholic Church volunteers fry over eighty thousand *fasnachts* (they form them into dough rings) to sell for charity.

No matter the disputes about the shape or the arguments about how best to eat them, the one thing the Pennsylvania Dutch can agree on is that *fastnachts* are indispensable for Mardi Gras, just as they are on the banks of the Rhine. Admittedly, the folks in Lancaster County didn't traditionally go in for the macabre celebrations of some of their German cousins, but that didn't mean they would sit home and pout. Fat Tuesday was long celebrated by public dances or "*fastnacht* frolics." Sounds like a great way to burn off all those sugar-dusted carbs!

Of course when you hear "Mardi Gras," you don't think Pennsylvania. It's New Orleans that comes to mind. Here too dough traditions have been mingling and crossbreeding for generations. The melt-in-your-mouth African American rice fritter called callas is one happy result. The New Orleans beignet is another. It was French settlers expelled from Atlantic Canada who brought an early form of these beloved fritters, which they called *croxignolles* (the spelling varies). Presumably they were the same shape as the cruller-like pastries or *croquinoles* that still occasionally crop up in rural Quebec. But that's quite different from the square donut found in Louisiana today. This contemporary version is described as far back as 1885 by Lafcadio Hearn, who tells you to roll out his yeast-raised "doughnut" dough "a little thicker than pie dough and cut with a knife in squares of about three inches." A few years later the popular *Picayune Creole Cookbook* instructed readers to do much the same thing to achieve a "true Creole 'Croxignolle,'" or what New Orleanians would now call a beignet.

It turns out that New Orleans's signature fritter resembles Pennsylvania German donuts more than its French Canadian cousins. This is not as strange as it might at first seem. As in Pennsylvania, Germans arrived in Louisiana in the 1700s, from more or less the same part

At New Orleans's Café du Monde, the locals still prefer beignets to donuts and smooth out their coffee with a soupçon of chicory.

of the fatherland. More waves of *Fastnachtkuchen*-munching immigrants arrived after 1803 when Jefferson purchased Louisiana for the Union. So many arrived, in fact, that for most of the eighteen hundreds, every tenth New Orleanian was a German. It's perfectly plausible that their version of the donut was naturalized with a French name. Even today, bakeries with German names still supply the city with its indispensable French bread, Mardi Gras king cakes, and pies. And let's not forget Alois Binder Bakery with its square "German-Style" donuts. New Orleans's most famous beignet stops used to have a German connection too. Café du Monde, founded in 1862, was once owned by the Koenigers, and Morning Call was opened by Joseph Jurisich in 1870.

Both of these donut and coffee stalls originally stood in or near the French Market. By the 1880s this was the neighborhood to get a cheap, filling meal day or night. According to a contemporary guidebook, there were fancy ones called cafés where "the very best people" would stop by and sip on coffee or chocolate and nibble on a cookie or cake. There were also more ordinary restaurants. Here, if you ordered a meal, you'd get bread and donuts for free, though if all you wanted was coffee and donuts, it would set you back five cents. Those were the days.

## EARLY RECIPES

No matter their origin, most of America's earliest donuts were made with a lightly sweetened yeast dough, resulting in what we call a "raised donut" today. Sometimes the mixture was little more than bread dough enriched with butter and sugar. You'd roll it out and cut it or form it into whatever shape you pleased before frying. In New England, where wheat flour wasn't always available, they'd sometimes make do with rye, and molasses was often substituted for sugar in the days when a pound of that precious tropical commodity cost an ordinary worker's day's wage.

The very first American recipe in print comes from an appendix inserted by a New York publisher into a popular English cookbook to give the book a marketing edge. Susannah Carter's *The Frugal Housewife* hit the booksellers just in time for the 1802 Christmas shopping season, with a seventy-five-cent cover price. The gimmick of including recipes "adapted to the American mode of cooking" must have worked, because three years later, an Alexandria, Virginia, publisher lifted the appendix word for word and stuck it into an entirely different British recipe collection originally penned by Hannah Glasse.

These identical American appendices read like a what's what of colonial cookery, though with a decidedly New England accent. There's pumpkin pie and Indian pudding,

## DEATH BY DONUT

Before the arrival of automation in the 1920s, donuts were mostly a homemade treat, something that presented real danger to even experienced cooks. In 1897, the *New York Times* reported that a North Adams, Massachusetts, woman was burned to death when a kettle of fat, in which she had been frying donuts, overturned. Less lethal injuries must have been all too common. In 1870, the *Chicago Tribune* reported on an exploding donut, "deluging...the face and clothing of [its victim] with a gallon of red-hot lard." And how many other accidents never made the news?

buckwheat pancakes and cranberry tarts, maple sugar and maple beer. And there is a recipe for "dough nuts" and "crullers." The crullers are essentially fried sugar cookies made in "what form you please," while the dough nuts are made of the sort of enriched bread dough mentioned above. As with the crullers, the shape was up to you, so presumably there were already lots of variations by this point. Mary Randolph, the Southern author who reproduced the Carter recipe some two decades later, wasn't as permissive. She directs her readers to make these "Yankee" cakes the size of a half dollar (about 1½ inches in diameter), which would make them little bigger than a walnut. In his 1828 dictionary, the Yankee born-and-bred Noah Webster defined the "dough-nut" as a "small roundish cake, made of flour, eggs and sugar, moistened with milk and boiled in lard." When you put it that way, the name makes perfect sense.

When properly made, yeast-raised donuts have the kind of pillowy ethereality that make Krispy Kreme cultists experience the rapture. But they can also resemble greasy hockey pucks. Yeast used to be fiddly stuff for the domestic cook and not always convenient if you just wanted to cook up a quick batch of donuts. When Europeans first arrived in the New World, one of their frustrations was that the flour milled from indigenous corn couldn't be made into bread, in part because it lacked the gluten that yeast needs to do its heavy lifting. Eventually American cooks learned that when you mix certain chemicals (an alkali and an acid), carbon dioxide is produced. Depending on the exact chemicals, the alkali element was called pearlash (because it was derived from ashes) or saleratus ("aerating salt"). Mix a little buttermilk or another acid into one of these, add a little heat, and your cake would rise in a snap. While this technique was surely known since colonial days (a pearlash-leavened ginger-bread appears in the first American-written cookbook, published in 1796) it's hard to know when the first cook got the idea to use it in donuts.

The very first recipe for what we now know as cake donuts appears in 1829 in the first edition of Lydia Maria Child's *Frugal Housewife*. Her recipe must have been as sweet as a high-octane Twinkie—she calls for a pint of flour and a half pint of sugar with a teaspoonful of pearlash providing the lift. Later renamed *The American Frugal Housewife*, the Boston author's little volume eventually went through at least thirty-five printings by 1850. Many pioneers packed the highly portable guide to thrifty New England cooking when they headed west, taking the recipe for cake donuts with them. Making chemically leavened donuts became even easier when commercial baking powder was introduced by England's Borwick's Baking Powder Company in 1842 and quickly replicated by American manufacturers. Yet despite the ease of this new-fangled method of making fry cakes, there were some who couldn't abide the innovation. Consequently, cake and raised donuts duked it out in American cookbooks for generations.

## THE HOLEY DONUT

There was one thing missing though. While all these fry cakes were certainly donut-like, they aren't exactly the donut-shaped objects of Homer Simpson's daydreams. Early American donut recipes, if they even bother to mention it, often tell you to make the dough in "what shape you please" as the appendix to Susannah Carter's *Frugal Housewife* puts it. Philadelphia-based Eliza Leslie recommends using a pastry wheel to cut out diamonds. (The technique sounds like it might have been lifted from Friederike Löffler, which isn't entirely surprising, given that elsewhere Leslie describes donuts as "a German cake.") Others suggest using a wineglass to cut out a circle. But where's the hole? After all, isn't that what sets the American donut apart from all those other greaseballs?

If you ever happen to be in Rockport, Maine, consider making a detour to the Nativity Lutheran Church. There's a plaque there that pays tribute to the Edison of the donut hole erected here on the centenary of his purported breakthrough. "In commemoration," the weather-worn tribute reads, "this is the birthplace of Captain Hanson Gregory who first

Whether Captain Gregory invented the hole or not, this rare photo of the donut Columbus gives the impression that he had eaten his fair share of the pastry rings.

invented the hole in the donut in the year 1847." The world at large had first learned of the momentous feat in the spring of 1916, when the then eighty-five-year-old captain recounted the event to a reporter from the *Boston Post*. "It was way back—oh I don't know just what year…well I guess it was about '47, when I was 16," the old salt recalled, "that I was aboard ship and discovered the hole which was later to revolutionize the doughnut industry." Here's the rest of the yarn:

Now in them days we used to cut the doughnuts into diamond shapes, and also into long strips, bent in half, and then twisted. I don't think we called them doughnuts then—they was just "fried cakes" and "twisters."

Well, sir, they used to fry all right around the edges, but when you had the edges done, the insides was all raw dough. And the twisters used to sop up all the grease just where they bent, and they were tough on the digestion.

Well, I says to myself, "Why wouldn't a space inside solve the difficulty?" I thought at first I'd take one of the strips and roll it around, then I got an inspiration. I took the cover off the ship's tin pepper box, and—I cut into the middle of that doughnut the first hole even seen by mortal eyes!

When the teenage wunderkind returned to his hometown, Camden, he shared his discovery with his aged mother, and next thing you know, the innovation was scattered to the four winds. With a tinge of regret, Gregory added, "Well, I never took out a patent on it; I don't suppose Peary could patent the north pole or Columbus patent America."

The story gained so much currency that, in 1941, a great debate was staged at New York's swank Hotel Astor to determine its veracity. The occasion was the first annual convention of the National Dunking Association, an organization devoted to matters donut. On one side of the argument was Fred Crocket, Captain Gregory's great-grandnephew, defending his family honor, while Chief High Eagle of the Wampanoag tribe represented the dissenting view. The Native American tale involved a distant ancestor in pursuit of a Puritan

*THE DONUT*

housewife's donut. Whether the brave was after just her pastry remained unsaid, but whatever his motivations, he apparently shot an arrow that pierced the unholey fry cak e she held in her hand, creating the first hole. But the white men of the Dunking Association remained unconvinced; the delegates voted three to one to declare Gregory the Columbus of the pastry with a hole in the memorable year of 1847.

But was he? If the old sea dog invented the donut hole, he had a lot of company. The author of the *Every Lady's Book* suggests cutting crullers (though not donuts) into rings as early as 1844. In 1846, Mrs. Abell instructs the reader of her cookbook to cut her "fried cakes" (basically cake donuts) as you would jumbles, that is, ring-shaped cookies. There were surely others; there's no shortage of torus-shaped pastries around the globe.

The logic of opening up the center of a fry cake is irrefutable. As our inventive sailor points out, the fritter cooks much more quickly, so it is unlikely the center will remain raw. While the slashing method used by the Pennsylvania Dutch and some of their European cousins works well with a springy yeast-based dough, it would hardly do for more fragile cake dough. Thus an alternative had to be found, and

## THE DONUT HOLE

As early as 1904, the *New York Sun* pointed out: "'Twixt optimist and pessimist/The difference is droll;/The optimist the doughnut sees—/The pessimist the hole." In 1943, a *New York Times* reporter heard President Franklin D. Roosevelt musing, "Some people, when a doughnut is placed before them, claim they can see only the hole in it." That description might neatly describe early twenty-first-century economists who coined the term "donut hole" to characterize a gap in Medicare coverage when the legislation was updated a few years back.

Those in the donut biz tend to see the upside. After all, you can resell the donut hole, either by rerolling it into another sinker or frying it and selling it as is. When Dunkin' Donuts first introduced its donut holes in 1972, they were initially concerned that it would cannibalize their regular sales, but with a little marketing magic, they found they could have their cake and eat it too. When they named their minipastries Munchkins (after the *Wizard of Oz* characters), they discovered that kids clamored for them.

the jumble was the perfect model. These rolled, ring-shaped cookies had been around for generations. Some New Englanders even used the term *jumble,* or a variant, *cymbal,* as a synonym for a ring-shaped donut.

## DOING THE TWIST

If you think donuts have a complex history, crullers offer an even more twisted tale. Even the name, which most trace to the Dutch, could conceivably be traced to medieval English, when *crull* was just a variant of *curl.* Then there's the question of shape and recipe. Just trying to distinguish between a cruller and a donut is fraught with pitfalls.

In 1907, the *New York Times* expressed concern that the cruller-donut controversy might have led to a faux pas of international import. The occasion was that year's visit of Prince William of Sweden, who, upon his arrival, was subjected to a whirlwind of social engagements. He lunched with President Teddy Roosevelt, got wined and dined by Newport millionaires, and was cheered by a crowd of ten thousand when he visited the New York Stock Exchange. At one point he was so tired of it all that he snuck off to visit Coney Island. However, that's not what got the Grey Lady's goat. Apparently, on the eve of his final departure on the Swedish battle cruiser *Flygia,* the lanky twenty-three-year-old royal was spotted at the railway station in Pittsfield, Massachusetts, eating donuts. Or, had his Yankee hosts pulled one over on the prince and fed him crullers instead, as the *Times*'s correspondent feared? "Up in Maine a cruller is a doughnut; and in Massachusetts their comprehension of a doughnut is uncertain," the reporter worried, before giving the definition of each. "A doughnut contains some yeast, or, in these degenerate days, baking powder.... On the other hand, the cruller is made with eggs, and consists of shortened dough twisted around holes.

"We sadly fear," the writer fumed, "that Prince Wilhelm ate a cruller or two at Pittsfield, and will carry the memory of them back to Sweden to the great detriment of this great Republic."

In a subsequent letter to the editor, a New England reader commiserated with the correspondent's sentiment, though his reasoning differed. As far as he was concerned, Pittsfield was so close to New York State that its fried cakes weren't worth eating, no matter the name.

He ended his note by noting, "An Eastern Massachusetts man would not insult the pigs, if [he] kept any, by feeding them with New York doughnuts." If poor William had known of the controversy a lump of fried dough could engender, he might have stayed on his battle cruiser.

But the cruller dispute wouldn't die. Decades later, after solving the donut hole dispute, the dunkers who had convened at the Hotel Astor in 1941 made a stab at remedying this "bitter controversy in the doughnut ranks."

"The resolution offered by Alfred L. Plant, vice president of the association," the *Times* reported, "defines a doughnut as a 'circle of cake dough cooked in shortening to a golden brown.' A cruller, on the other hand, is 'an elongated piece of dough, straight or twisted.'"

As if a resolution by a bunch of Manhattan upstarts could calm the boiling fat of generations! In 1943, an exasperated "Connecticut housewife" found it necessary to correct the ignorance shown by the fry cake worthies at the Hotel Astor. Citing the wisdom of Jane Putnam, one of her great-grandmothers, she writes to the *New York Times*:

> Doughnuts are made of pieces of raised dough, cut into circular pieces and set to rise. After rising they are dropped into a kettle of hot fat, where they puff up into balls and become brown on the surface. Crullers and fried cakes, on the other hand, are made of dough leavened with baking powder—in colonial times soda served instead.
>
> For fried cakes, frequently misnamed as doughnuts and crullers, the dough is rolled out and cut into circles, and then a smaller circle is cut out of the center of each cake. It is the fried cake that has the hole. The cruller is twisted or curled.

The fact is, the line between donuts and crullers has always been hard to draw with any certainty, and even crullers vary enormously among themselves. Roughly speaking, a cruller could be one of three things. The earliest recipes, like the one in the Carter appendix, were little more than fried sugar cookies, the "crisp and crumbling cruller" as Washington Irving memorably described the Dutch version of the treat. According to Eliza Leslie, these could be twisted "into various fantastic shapes." You still find similar crunchy confections in Spain and North Africa, even if they are less "fantastic" than the Philadelphia guru of domesticity

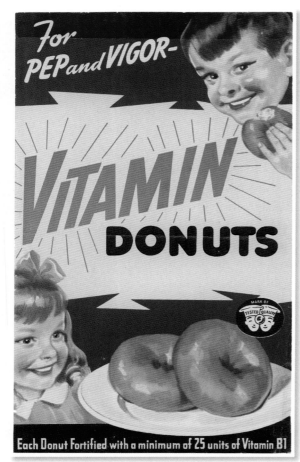

For PEP and VIGOR—
VITAMIN DONUTS

Each Donut Fortified with a minimum of 25 units of Vitamin B1

The Doughnut Corporation of America sought endorsement from the Nutrition Division of the War Food Administration for its Vitamin Donuts campaign.

envisioned. Other crullers have used a sort of cream puff dough. Leslie called these "soft crullers" and had you pass the dough through something she describes as a screw funnel. In essence these were descendants of English syringed fritters. Later in the century, people started calling them "French crullers," probably not because they were originally French but rather because anything French used to be fancy. And fancy they are. A good French cruller is almost greaseless, hitting a sweet spot somewhere between delicate and toothsome with effortless charm. The third kind of cruller is really nothing more than an upwardly mobile donut—perhaps eggier and sweeter than your average sinker but always with a twist.

## DONUTS DO DENVER

By the end of the Civil War—if not earlier—most of the donuts we know and love had made themselves at home in the American larder. Some had gone west with New Englanders looking for a better life. Others were introduced to the reading public through East Coast cookbooks and magazines. As they became naturalized, the fry cakes picked up a little Southern twang here and a Midwestern accent there. Soon enough, regionally popular cookbooks, like Ohio's *Buckeye Cookery,* would include a half dozen cake donut variations along with a raised version for the old-timers.

Even way out west, in the Colorado Rockies, the miners burrowing into the mountains at Leadville had a thing for donuts. In the 1870s, according to Jessup Whitehead, a prolific food writer of the time, the prospectors were especially fond of something called the "Little Pittsburg," named after the most prominent local silver strike. This was an old-style sinker made by stirring some lard, sugar, and eggs into bread dough. "You could get a Little

Pittsburg doughnut for ten cents at any hour of the day and night, and a glass of dried-apple cider for the same price," Whitehead writes. "So little Pittsburg doughnuts became a part, and indeed, a leading feature of the camp."

The bakery would scatter short advertisements throughout the local paper, and, because ads and articles were barely distinguishable in those days, it occasionally made for peculiar copy. At the top of the column you read: "Our esteemed fellow citizen fell down a shaft 500 feet deep, last evening. He struck on his head and probably never knew what hurt him." And then: "O! those Little Pittsburg doughnuts are so very fine, if you try them once you'll buy them every time, at the Union Bakery."

By the end of the nineteenth century, donuts had become a popular treat across the USA. Here cooks and their helpers take a donut break in Oregon.

However, at the extraordinary price of ten cents a pop (three dollars was a common daily wage) there was plenty of room for competition, and soon enough, the donut carpetbaggers moved in. They could make their sinkers bigger or cheaper and still be rolling in dough. As a result the Union Bakery's business model caved in. In Whitehead's donut-centric view of the matter, the demise of the once-beloved institution and its withdrawal from the ad market presaged a disaster for all: "None may know what subtle connection there may be in the cases, but both the Leadville newspapers soon after died, and the Little Pittsburgh mine itself experienced a temporary collapse."

Yet Colorado would hardly be the fry cake's final frontier. In 1900, *Harper's* related the donut's conquest of the great white north. In the hardscrabble existence of the Klondike gold prospector, donuts weren't merely a toothsome treat; they could be a lifesaver. "Doughnuts are all important to the man who goes on trail for a journey of any length," the New York magazine writer reports. "Bread freezes easily and there is less grease and sugar, and hence less heat in it, than in doughnuts. The latter do not solidify except at extremely low temperatures, and they are very handy to carry in the pockets of a Mackinaw jacket and munch as one travels along. They are made much after the manner of their brethren in warmer climes, with

## DONUTS AND HEALTH

Over the years, there has been some dissent regarding the donut's role in a healthy diet. Writing in 1838, the prolific killjoy William Alcott deplored all cakes as "generally objectionable," though he considered donuts among the least offensive of the bunch. Some fifty years on, the phys ed crusader Edward Hitchcock was less forgiving, classing donuts among "the poisons of the farmer's life." On the other hand, the professors of medicine who penned the 1919 *Diet in Health and Disease* suggested that donuts be included in the diet of the United States Government Hospital for the Insane. So just how bad could they be?

Perhaps the greatest proponent of the donut diet was the delightfully named Dr. Howard J. Crumb. The good doctor had a way with publicity. In 1931, he performed what was billed as the first ever public face-lift when he operated on the face of "motion picture player" Martha Pettel before an audience of more that six hundred cosmetologists attending a Philadelphia beauty convention. By 1937, he'd moved on to donuts as a prescription for a svelte figure. "Take the word of Dr. Howard J. Crum [*sic*]," the AP reported, "coffee and doughnut is proper fare for seekers of slenderness. Years of experimenting with reducing diets have proved the time-honored combination to be most satisfactory, he told the Southern Beauticians Association." I can't say the diet has worked for me, but it has done wonders for my mental health!

the exception that they are cooked in bacon grease—the more grease the better they are." It wouldn't be the first (or the last) time donuts were used as a survival ration.

By the turn of the twentieth century, the pastry with a hole could be found from sea to shining sea. To a few, the greasy treat still retained some of its cranky New England personality, but to most it had lost any regional association. The donut became as American as Mom and considerably more so than apple pie. It was a little ungainly and occasionally comical, beloved by many and denounced by a few. Yet its golden age was still before it. Many historians have called the twentieth century the American century. I would add that it was also the century of the donut, and no, that's not a coincidence. If you want to understand American dominance in the last hundred years, you'd do well to get to know the donut. And if you think I'm off my rocker, just ask the doughboys who fought in the trenches of World War I.

# 3

# DONUTS OF LORE
# AND LEGEND

## DONUTS FOR DOUGHBOYS

In the spring of 1918, the Germans, in a series of failed offensives, tried to turn the tide of a war that was inexorably washing their imperial ambitions out to sea. Increasingly desperate, their assault was merciless. On Easter Sunday they targeted a Salvation Army truck that had become stalled about a mile back of American lines. Why? Because the vehicle was full of donuts and pies intended as a holiday treat for the boys in the trenches. Hoping to convince Johnny to march right back home, the Axis commanders gave it everything they'd got. First, they sent up eight balloons to calibrate the range, and then they proceeded to pound the truck with long-range artillery day after day after day. On Tuesday night, a hundred GIs volunteered to try to rescue the pastries but had to turn back in the face of the shellfire and gas. Finally, on Wednesday morning, after an expenditure of many hundreds of shells, the kaiser's artillery blew the truck to smithereens, sending a rain of crumbs across the western front. Their vengeance exhausted, the guns fell silent.

Reporting the story, the *New York Times* noted, "The plight of the Easter doughnuts and pies was known all over the American sector, and the news of their loss today was received with the keenest regret all along the line." And little wonder. In World War I, the Salvation

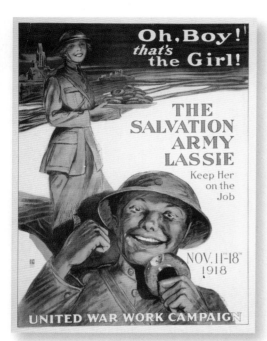

The Salvation Army used every means at its disposal to promote its cause.

Army's donuts were more than just a pleasant interruption in the onslaught of blood, mud, and guts; donuts came to represent mom and country—an edible symbol of what the servicemen were fighting for.

## ARMY LASSIES

The story of how the fried dough circles took on such a pivotal role in the Salvation Army's mission on the Western Front has the ring of the miracle of the loaves and fishes. When the United States joined the war to end all wars in 1917, the Salvation Army and other charities followed the doughboys into the muddy fields of northern France. (Incidentally, the term "doughboys" dates to the Mexican-American War of 1846–48 and has nothing to do with donuts.) Before shipping overseas, the Salvation Army's female volunteers were steeled for the ordeal by their superiors. There was the danger of the shells, of course, but there was a more pressing threat to the young women's virtue. Commander Evangeline Booth directed the young women to "put away the arts and coquetries of youth," a daunting task given that they would soon be wading into fields of testosterone-fueled postadolescents.

One of the earliest Salvation Army outposts was some 150 miles east of Paris and 20 miles behind the front in the village of Montiers-sur-Saulx. The New York office had arranged two circus tents to be sent over to serve as the army's HQ. Back home, the Salvation Army was known for its street theater, marching bands, and popular hymns. Soon enough they were organizing much the same in French village squares, where they found a ready audience among the uniformed men, who were none too eager to meet their maker. While this sort of pious entertainment was better than nothing, it couldn't make up for the shells or the pestilential weather. As Evangeline Booth tells it in her poetically augmented annals of war, "It had been raining steadily for thirty-six days, making swamps and pools everywhere. Depression like a great heavy blanket hung over the whole area." Then heavenly inspiration struck.

The way the diaries of Ensign Margaret Sheldon tell it is a little more prosaic: she and her comrade Adjutant Helen Purviance had gotten the notion that donuts would make a nice change from the pies, cocoa, and fudge they'd been making for the boys. So, in late September 1917, they got ahold of the ingredients for a batch of dough. According to army records, the honor of frying the first donut fell to Purviance. It turned out to be the first of many. Soon enough, all the lassies, as the women came to be called, were making donuts by the thousands. The women improvised as they could, rolling out the donuts with a grape juice bottle, cutting them out with a baking powder can, and poking out the holes with a funnel. They sold the fried rings at cost (and often on credit) for about twenty cents a half dozen. As the Christmas of 1917 approached, Sheldon jotted down in her diary, "I made fifty-six pies and 1,500 d'nuts and they went fine. Then on Sat. I made fifty pies and 2,000 d'nuts." The ensign estimated that she cooked more than a million donuts before the war was out.

As the conflict dragged on, the Salvation Army's pie and donut dispensaries multiplied, and their contribution to American morale grew ever more critical. Despite the war shortages, the American high command made sure the flour and lard for the donuts got through, even if they sometimes needed a little reminder. There was usually the will and even the money, but there weren't always supplies. Certainly the local market was no use. The French were surviving on black bread made of barley flour and other donut-unfriendly ingredients. The only place to get the necessary sugar, flour, and lard was through the US Army commissary. Luckily, the lassies hadn't entirely put away their arts and coquetries; they knew that the way to a man's heart—even if he happened to be wearing a general's uniform—was through his stomach.

Running low on supplies, a Salvation Army adjutant decided to go to the source. The lassies supplied him with a dozen apple pies, twelve hundred freshly baked donuts, and one big gorgeous chocolate cake, which he packed into a rough army truck that he drove to the local American Expeditionary Force headquarters. The general was thoroughly pleased with his cake, as were all the officers whose palms were greased with the oily pastries, so pleased in fact, that as the adjutant was leaving, he discovered seven tons of flour, sugar, and lard being loaded into his rusty vehicle.

The Salvation Army had long had unorthodox ways of getting things done, something that hadn't always endeared it to the American mainstream. This changed dramatically during the war. Theodore Roosevelt Jr. (the former president's son) spoke for many when he wrote of his service in France, "Before the war I felt that the Salvation Army was composed of a well-meaning lot of cranks. Now what help I can give them is theirs. My feelings are well illustrated by a conversation I overheard between two soldiers. One said, 'Say, Bill, before this war I used to think it good fun to kid the Salvation Army. Now I'll bust any feller on the bean with a brick if I see him botherin' them.'" Donuts had a lot to do with it. "The American soldiers take their hats off to the Salvation Army," wrote a correspondent for the *New York Times* in 1918, "and when the memoirs of this war come to be written the doughnuts and apple pies of the Salvation Army are going to take their place in history."

Today, it's hard to fully appreciate the importance of the Salvation Army's presence in the trenches, in part because government has taken over many of the roles charitable and/or religious organizations used to take on. Today, it's army psychologists who deal with morale, and if the US army were looking to provide donuts to the troops, they would likely turn to a slick military contractor—which would no doubt charge the American taxpayer twenty-four-karat prices for the glazed rings.

The lassies had no need of any of that; they had God and a dress code that almost guaranteed the soldiers wouldn't violate the young women's sacred donut mission. If you stop to think about it, the holey objects of desire were as loaded with symbolism as they were with hog fat. Anthropologists have long recognized the perforated circle as a symbol of fertility and feminine sexuality—the female analog of the phallus. In some cases, this is explicit, such as in the ring-shaped, plaited, and egg-encrusted cakes traditional for Easter throughout the Mediterranean, but it's true of other holey pastries as well. And it's not just tenured academics who hold this opinion; just look under *donut* in any dictionary of slang. I'm not the only one who sees something distinctly suggestive about young women distributing circle-shaped snacks to men clutching their well-oiled, bayonet-tipped rifles.

Needless to say, this is not a reading Commander Booth would have condoned. She tells the story of a young adjutant (presumably Helen Purviance) who gave the donuts a much more maternal spin: "[I]nvariably the boys would begin to talk about home and mother while they were eating the doughnuts. Through the hole in the doughnut they seemed to see the mother's face, and as the doughnut disappeared it grew bigger and clearer." For the purposes of their sanity, it was probably easier for the soldiers to think of the young women as mother or at least sister figures rather than the alternative. That was certainly the way the Salvation Army's Colonel William Barker explained it to a reporter from the *Boston Daily Globe*:

> [The donuts] put pep into every doughboy. Every doughboy felt his mother was somewhere just back of the lines in the midnight mists and damps—frying doughnuts for him just as she used to do, and the Germans noticed the improved morale of the Yankees.
>
> The round, jolly-faced, homely apple pie and the laughing, golden brown doughnuts shouldered the rifles and fought like—well the Spirit of '76 at Chateau Thierry and St. Mihiel [two prominent World War I battles].

Eventually the Lassies got such "high-tech" gear as rolling pins and donut cutters.

It's easy to forget that the lassies weren't in France merely to provide a morale booster. Many of them genuinely believed they were on a spiritual or religious quest. The donuts weren't just a sideline, they were part and parcel of the mission. As an editorial in an early edition of the *War Cry*, the Salvationist newspaper, explained, "The genius of the Army has been...that it has religionized secular things...it has brought religion out of the clouds into everyday life, and has taught the world that we may and ought to be as religious about our eatings and drinkings and dressing as we are about our prayings." In much the way that the army had earlier converted tavern songs into hymns, during the war, the lassies transubstantiated donuts into a kind of spiritual host. In the way they saw it, the coffee and donuts they handed out weren't so different from the eatings and drinkings of a Christian mass.

Despite the fact that no more than about 250 Salvationists actually served in France, the lassies with their donuts became the organization's calling card. The donut girls were not only featured in Salvation Army posters, but they became an icon of popular culture. Tin Pan Alley celebrated the lassies in popular tunes. Commander Booth even encouraged it,

## THE CHORUS TO "MY DOUGHNUT GIRL"

Don't forget the Salvation Army,
Always remember my doughnut girl.
She brought them doughnuts and coffee.
Just like an angel, she was their best pal.
As brave as a lion but meek as a lamb.
She carried on beside the sons of Uncle Sam.
So don't forget the Salvation Army,
Remember my doughnut girl.

*Words by Elmore Leffingwell and James Lucas*
*Broadway Music Corporation, 1919*

allowing the sheet music of "My Doughnut Girl" to be endorsed with the Salvation Army's official seal.

She also took advantage of plays and movies to promote her brand. When Paramount Pictures proposed to film a tearjerker to be called *Fires of Faith*, the commander plunged right in, even agreeing to play herself in several scenes. Sadly, the film is gone. Apparently it was a cookie-cutter melodrama in which a young innocent is seduced by a dastardly cad before finding redemption in the Salvation Army. The legendary producers Adolf Zukor and Jessie Lasky, made sure to include just enough sin in the plotline to draw in the crowds and came up with a variety of promotional gimmicks to grab the attention of the press. For the film's New York premiere, the producers set up the stage to look like a French field hospital. Before the screening, an image of a stained-glass window was projected on the back curtain even as in the foreground a Red Cross nurse tended to wounded soldiers. As the nurse departed, a Salvation Army lassie strode on stage bearing a pan of donuts. She distributed the sinkers to the bed-ridden men, then stepped into the spotlight to sing an eponymous song dedicated to the silent movie. Once the movie left Manhattan, some local distributors took it into their own hands to mount a publicity campaign worthy of *Shrek 4*. Upstate in Poughkeepsie, New York, a theater owner got local businesses involved. Bakeries promoted the feature with posters and discounted donuts. One drugstore put a *Fires of Faith* sundae on its menu, while another featured a drink-and-donut special named for one of the film's stars.

You might say that the donut, through its association with the Salvation Army, was born again. Donut chains such as Mayflower and, a little later, Krispy Kreme sprang up to feed America's appetite for the celebrity dough rings. Companies the likes of Belshaw, Dono, and the Doughnut Corporation of America devised ways to automate the production of the hitherto handmade pastries. (More on that later.) Taking note of the sinker's rise in 1920, the advertising industry's trade paper *Printer's Ink* wrote, "The doughnut . . . was reborn near the fighting front—a 'war baby' tenderly mothered by the brave lassies of the Salvation Army. . . . The derided doughnut was vindicated. It became the national, if not indeed the international epitome of the appetizing and the satisfying in the menu of handy snacks."

The army kept using sinkers to raise dough for its mission right through the Roaring Twenties and the Great Depression. The lassies distributed some three thousand donuts to US veterans in 1927 in Paris on the tenth anniversary of America's declaration of war. Following the stock market crash of

In the interwar years, the Salvation Army came up with all sorts of donut-based gimmicks like this donut-eating contest to raise money for the charity.

1929, the Salvation Army mobilized for battle on the home front. Once again, donuts and coffee multiplied like loaves and fishes, though this time not in Flanders's fields but on skid rows across America. In a little over a month in the winter of 1934, the organization's canteens broke all previous records by distributing two and a half million donuts and a million and a half cups of coffee to needy New Yorkers. Throughout the 1920s, the Salvation Army would organize "doughnut days," when volunteers sold donuts on street corners to raise funds for the charity. After a lag of some years, the fund-raising tactic was revived in Chicago in June 1938 to raise money for a home for unmarried mothers, though on this occasion the only donuts that exchanged hands were made out of cardboard. This event eventually became a template for a "National Doughnut Day" subsequently held the first Friday of each June. With the coming of World War II, the organization once again began to prep its fry kettles,

The Salvation Army wasn't the only one looking for converts during the Depression. Looking to burnish his Robin Hood reputation, Al Capone set up his own donut dispensary.

but this time they would no longer play the leading role. Although the Salvation Army still contributed donuts by the millions to the war effort, at the front lines, the lassie was jilted for a newer, younger companion in arms.

## CLUBMOBILE GIRLS

With the coming of the winter of 1943, the allied invasion of Italy didn't look as promising as it had earlier that fall when Italy had surrendered. By December, the American advance was halted by Hitler's troops to the south of Rome in the hilly terrain near the ancient Benedictine monastery of Cassino. On Christmas Day, American GIs sat in their muddy foxholes with nothing to look forward to except a hail of fire and brimstone from the German guns across the hill and cans of C rations for their holiday dinner. Imagine the surprise when one of the servicemen turned around and spotted young Isabella Hughes of Baltimore, outfitted with a neat Red Cross uniform and a pretty smile, carrying a steaming pot of coffee in one hand and a box of donuts in the other.

"Good Lord, sweetheart! What are you doing here?" the soldier sputtered, according to a reporter on the scene.

Isabella gave the young man three donuts, a canteen full of coffee, an American magazine and—perhaps more crucially—a sense that there was another world worth fighting for outside of this rain-soaked hellhole. Along with two other members of her Red Cross team, she served thirteen thousand donuts to more than five thousand soldiers that Christmas Day.

Isabella was just one of many thousands of Red Cross volunteers who risked their lives to bring coffee and donuts to the boys on the front. The role of the volunteer organization had shifted between the wars. During World War I, the Red Cross was better known for its hospital work than donuts, though the charity did engage in some nonmedical welfare work, joining organizations such as the Knights of Columbus, YMCA, Jewish Welfare Board, and, of course, the Salvation Army. After Pearl Harbor, the American Armed Forces took control of the medical services. They still depended on the Red Cross to provide nurses and collect blood, but mostly the charity was charged with making the war just a little less hellish for the soldiers abroad. Overseas, it was the young women volunteers who had to do most of the heavy lifting.

Before they'd be accepted for their demanding and often dangerous assignment, the "girls" (who had to be over twenty-five to join up) were carefully screened stateside by the Red Cross. They had to have the right wholesome look, be able to talk about Main Street and Broadway, discuss the lineup for the Red Sox and Cubs, but most especially know how to deflect a catcall. They had to dole out wisecracks along with the donuts. Once in Europe there was no getting away from the boys. "If you have a club foot, buck teeth, crossed eyes, and a cleft palate, you can still be Miss Popularity," Elizabeth Richardson, a Red Cross volunteer wrote home in 1944. "The main thing is that you're female and speak English. It's certain that all of us will have more than a workable knowledge of the ways of men. 'Men, men, men,' one of my co-workers was heard to exclaim the other night, 'I hope I never see another,'—a vain hope, as she no doubt knew." The young women tried their best to maintain some sort of standard despite the dust and the muck and the lack of sanitary facilities in the field. It wasn't easy. In many cases they couldn't bathe for days. All too often they had to fill up their helmets with water to wash their hair. Their hands were red and raw from the weather and the frying and the cleaning. Then there was the "eau de doughnut," as Richardson characterized the odor of stale grease that permeated them to the very core. Men being men, this didn't exactly turn out to be a chastity belt; several unmarried Red Cross women had to be sent home when they became pregnant.

As part of their morale-boosting mission, the Red Cross set up clubs where soldiers on leave could get a night's sleep and a meal. These were, as one director of a London Red Cross Club put it, "not only a home away from home, but the fraternity house, the Elks Club, the corner drug store and Mom's front parlor all wrapped into one." (What he meant by "corner drug store" was that clubs were a convenient place to pick up a pack of condoms.)

Later the Red Cross took the show on the road, adapting trucks to serve as barebones versions of the stationary clubs. By 1944, there were more than a hundred of these "Club-mobiles" in operation in Europe, North Africa, and the Persian Gulf. Except in the Middle

American Red Cross clubmobiles reminded GIs on the battlefront what they were fighting for.

East, they were operated, and often driven, by the Red Cross "girls." The units were equipped with all the essentials: a phonograph, a movie setup, books, magazines, and the indispensable donut machine. The young women gave the vehicles patriotic names like Old Glory and Abraham Lincoln or called them Kansas City and Nebraska as a reminder of home. Where the lassies of World War I had to improvise with baking powder cans and grape juice bottles, the Clubmobiles were outfitted with Rube Goldberg-like automatic donut machines made by the Doughnut Corporation of America. (Have a look at chapter 4, for more on the DCA.) The company loaned the Red Cross 468 machines, each capable of cranking out forty-eight dozen sinkers an hour. The donation wasn't entirely altruistic though: the contract specified that the Red Cross had to buy all of its donut flour from the manufacturer. The mix, shipped across the Atlantic in barrels, was a combination of flour, sugar, egg and milk powders, baking powder, and salt. It only required the women to add water, which they were supposed to weigh out with great accuracy. The women, who couldn't have survived without a healthy sense of humor, emblazoned "We weigh the water" on issues of the Clubmobile newsletter, *The Sinker*.

Making donuts in the field involved dangers the girls never dreamed of back in Missouri. You get a vibrant glimpse of this in the letters and diaries of St. Louis native Mary Marshall Metcalfe. In snapshots, the former department store salesclerk sports a wholesome, toothy smile that couldn't always have been easy to maintain. Her Clubmobile, the Abraham Lincoln, was one of the first to cross the English Channel in the Normandy invasion. As the crew advanced into conquered territory, there were mines everywhere. On one occasion, a GI grabbed a donut and coffee but stepped on a hidden mine and was blown to kingdom come before he had a chance to take a bite. There was a night when the young women woke to bombs dropping to the vehicle's left and right. By dawn they were surrounded by craters twice the size of their truck. And, as if Hitler and his buzz bombs weren't bad enough, the volunteers also occasionally had to deal with rabid swarms of yellow jackets. Mary recalled an occasion when the soldiers could barely stuff the donuts into their mouths without ingesting the merciless insects. The mild-mannered Midwesterner noted, "Many new cuss words were added to their vocabularies and to ours. I was tempted to repeat some of them when, almost elbow-deep in dough, I was the target of eight painful stings."

As the trucks trudged from France to Germany, past rotting bodies and eviscerated villages, new kinds of problems cropped up. On one assignment, the girls were asked to take their truck ("greasy Abe" as they now called it) into an airbase near Halle that was full of newly released American POWs. Having survived months on the starvation diets of the Nazi camps, the boys had a hard time refraining from gorging themselves, even when their malnourished bodies couldn't handle it. As a rule, the army doctors forbade giving donuts to the emaciated soldiers, but they must have relented on this occasion, because Mary records delivering some four thousand donuts and 350 gallons of coffee to the liberated soldiers. It proved to be barely enough.

It was now the spring of 1945, and even while Hitler's dream of a thousand-year Reich was kaput, halfway around the world the carnage continued. Following the Allied victory in May, the United States started shipping soldiers to the Pacific front. However, there were inevitable bottlenecks. At Reims, France, hundreds of thousands of men at a time spent several weeks in a huge tent metropolis as they awaited space on the troop transports. The army command, fearful that this bored, sex-starved horde would cause havoc in the neighboring French cities, sent in the USO to perform no less than seventeen shows, and the Red Cross to serve its donuts. According to press reports the boys consumed a million cups of coffee and a half-million donuts each day. Supplying the mountains of necessary ingredients would have been a logistical nightmare in the best of circumstances, but that spring, as Atlantic supply lines clogged and food stocks in Europe dropped below needs, the War Department in Washington suggested cutting the shipments of lard, evaporated milk, sugar, and coffee destined for the Red Cross in half. But the army brass in France would have none of this. When they heard the news of this looming catastrophe, they let the Pentagon know in no uncertain terms that Red Cross coffee and donuts were critical to keeping up army morale. The donuts kept coming.

If the folks back home had any doubts of the contribution made by the Red Cross girls and their donuts in defeating the Nazi war machine, Dwight D. Eisenhower, the supreme commander of the Allies in Europe, spelled it out: "The Red Cross," Ike told a joint session of Congress in 1945, "with its clubs for recreation, its coffee and doughnuts in the forward areas, its readiness to meet the needs of the well and help minister to the wounded—even more important, the devotion and warmhearted sympathy of the Red Cross girl! The Red Cross has often seemed to be the friendly hand of this nation, reaching across the sea to sustain its fighting men."

## VICTORY AT HOME

The sinker, the veteran of foreign wars, the darling of the Western Front, the hero of the Italian campaign, was welcomed home with open arms. The Salvation Army lassies could certainly take a lot of credit for the improved standing of the all-American pastry. Yet even so, in 1918, the transformation wasn't complete. At the time, the donut still shared the stage with Mom and apple pie as embodiments of what the doughboys had fought for. By 1945, however, it almost stood alone. Though donut consumption numbers are about as reliable as a GI on leave, according to the Doughnut Corporation of America, we ate 1.26 billion donuts in 1933, 3.96 billion in 1939, and 7.2 billion in 1945, which, a donut demographer would tell you, means that we went from about ten donuts per person per year to about forty in the dozen intervening years. Whatever the real numbers, it's safe to say that following the Second World War, the climate was ideal for a donut golden age.

Among the returning vets, there were some who saw a business opportunity in the iconic pastry. The 1944 GI Bill not only offered free college tuition to returning veterans, but also guaranteed small business loans. Notices in *American Legion* magazine advertised discharged veterans an "opportunity in Donut Shops, not available right now to civilians" and urged them to send away for a brochure. The authors of *A Treatice* [sic] *on the Art of Donut Making* (1947) had the same idea. Their introduction notes, "This book has been written primarily because there are so many ambitious people in this country looking for a business of their own. There are ex-G.I.'s just out of the service that don't want to go back to their old job, working for someone else." Donuts were just the ticket.

Another effect of the GI Bill was that it made available cheap mortgages that stimulated a suburban building boom. America, once a place of country and city folk, rapidly transformed into something quite new. We became a nation of Levittown dwellers who drove Chevrolets to A&Ps where we bought Swansons to stock our Frigidaires and then consumed the contents of the aluminum trays before the warm glow of our RCAs. We became suburbanites. This had implications for donuts just as it did for every other hallowed American institution.

Like Jefferson's vision of America, the idea of the donut was long associated with the bucolic countryside, populated by mothers and wives who hand cut rings of sweet dough to nourish their hardworking menfolk. That doughty archetype persisted right through the First World War and even afterward when most of the menfolk were more likely to grab their sinker on the way to the factory than the farmyard. With the end of World War II, the myth of Mother's donuts was on life support, and by the 1950s, Mom was excised from the equation altogether. If she had anything to do with the fried pastries, she had most likely driven to pick them up at Dunkin' Donuts, Winchell's, or Krispy Kreme. Donuts were something anyone and everyone now purchased at the donut shop. Rather than being associated with motherhood and New England, the donut had acquired somewhat different connotations. The Depression, the Second World War, and the subsequent GI Bill had made the country much more egalitarian, a country of regular Janes and Joes, seemingly populated by the characters from the *Honeymooners* and the *Andy Griffith Show*. Like the most popular personalities on television, the donut came to be seen as decidedly ordinary, egalitarian, even democratic. It was the doughy everyman.

The director Frank Capra saw this as early as 1934 when he set up the ménage à trois of Claudette Colbert, Clark Gable, and an old-fashioned in the film *It Happened One Night*. Colbert, playing Ellie Andrews, a prissy heiress on the lam from her millionaire father, happens to get on an overnight bus with tabloid reporter Peter Warne, played by a young, handsome, and irrepressibly smart-ass Gable. The next morning, as they sit down to a breakfast of

In both World Wars, donuts were an essential component of the US war effort.

# DONUTS AND KENNEDY

So was he or wasn't he?

Academics and scandal-hungry gravediggers have unearthed great piles of dirt about the short life of the glamorous and tragic president. We now know all about his affair with Marilyn Monroe, his nearly addictive dependence on painkillers, and every excruciating second of the Cuban missile crisis. But what presidential historians really want to know is if the president was a jelly donut. Or at least if that's what he told the good people of West Berlin. And, if so, could this explain his success with women, or the envy of his Republican opponent, Richard Nixon?

Apparently it all hangs on a single article and a fine point of German grammar.

John Fitzgerald Kennedy assumed the presidency even as the Cold War was threatening to get too hot to handle. In 1961, the East Germans erected a wall around West Berlin to prevent their citizens from escaping into the American-controlled sector. Food was cut off too, so the enclave became dependent on supplies brought in by the planes—what would come to be known as the Berlin Airlift. Consequently when the president visited Berlin in 1963, it was no casual visit, and when, on June 26, he stood on a podium in front of Berlin's city hall, an audience of 150,000 hung on his every word. About a minute and half into the speech, the president looked down briefly at his notes and declared in his unmistakable Boston cadence, "Today's proudest boast is: Ish bin ein Bearleener." (His hand-written transcription of *"Ich bin ein Berliner,"* or "I am a Berliner.") The adoring crowd erupted with frenzied cheers, as they did when he repeated the phrase once again at the end of his address.

According to a respected journalist writing for the *New York Times*, the fatal grammatical error the president made was to insert the article before "Berliner."

As any high school German student knows, the proper phrase should have been *"Ich bin Berliner."* Once you insert the pronoun, you're a thing, a *Berliner*, as jelly donuts are known in parts of Germany. The journalist even adds the telltale detail that the audience tittered when they heard the famed orator proclaim that he was a jelly donut. Did I mention that the writer first noticed this in 1988, twenty-five years after the event? And he wasn't even there? It turns out that students of high school German may not be the best authority on this.

One eminent student of the German language became so annoyed with this urban legend that he wrote an entire academic paper on the subject. Jürgen Eichhoff is the author of over a dozen books on the German language, including a hyper-wonky, multivolume word atlas. And the Herr Doctor knows his donuts. His atlas includes a detailed map of the distribution of German dialect terms for the fried dough balls: people in Berlin do not call them *Berliners* (any more than the Viennese call their sausages Wieners or the French their fried potatoes French fries). They call them *Pfannkuchen*. And that story about the article? He says it's a lot of hooey—well not in exactly those words. Apparently once you've advanced beyond high school German, you discover that rules have their exceptions, and Kennedy, depending on a text penned by a native-speaking German and rehearsed in front of born and bred Berliners, got it just right. In the right context—that is if you're standing in front of a people tested and tried—*"Ich bin ein Berliner"* means, in very rough translation, "I am one of you; I feel as if I too am a Berliner." Maybe the question presidential historians really need to ask is if Kennedy got a chance to try a *Pfannkuchen*, and if so what did the New England, donut-raised president think of the local sinkers?

scrambled eggs, black coffee, and donuts, Peter looks on incredulously as Ellie picks up her sinker and buries it in the coffee cup. Smirking, he quips, "Say, where'd you learn to dunk? In finishing school?"

He goes on with a brief dissertation: "Dunking's an art. Don't let it soak so long. A dip and"—he demonstrates with the effortless gesture of the virtuoso, finishing the sentence with his mouth full—"plop, in your mouth. You let it hang there too long, it'll get soft and fall off. It's all a matter of timing. Aw, I oughta write a book about it." She laughs so we know that she's OK. We also know she's no snob because, to Peter's wisecrack that she may be worth $20 million but doesn't know how to dunk, she says, "Oh, I'd change places with a plumber's daughter any day." (Yeah right—only in the movies.) After numerous other plot twists that need not concern us since they don't involve donuts, the two eventually marry.

Sinkers have done well in times of financial crisis as well as war. You get a sense of this in the dramatic increase in donut consumption during the Great Depression. Something similar occurred under the dismal economic climate of the late 1970s, when donut franchises proliferated. It doesn't take a rocket scientist to figure out why. With its chubby contours and doughy texture, the donut is the ultimate comfort food: sweet and filling, a treat whether it's eaten as a snack or even as a meal. And, it bears repeating, donuts are cheap. To a blue-collar working stiff, sinkers were an affordable pleasure even in the worst of times.

This is not to say that the donut shops of the post–World War II era put out signs emblazoned with "Give me your tired, your poor, your huddled masses." The stores catered to anybody and everybody, but at certain times of day, the clientele was decidedly

Donut making was a tedious process until mechanization came along, and even then the donut bakers had little more than a hand-cranked device to make enough to feed the clamoring multitudes.

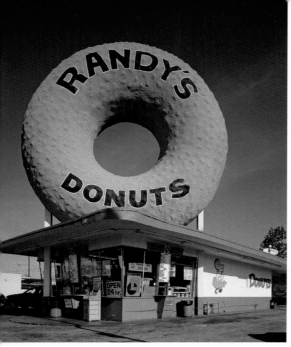

California may not have invented the donut, but it sure took it to a new height. Whether you were commuting to your shift at the plant or driving the kids home from baseball practice, who could miss it?

working class, especially in certain neighborhoods. In the days before the Egg McMuffin (introduced in 1972), there were hardly any restaurants open on the road in the wee hours of the morning other than donut shops. If you were coming off the late shift or heading to the early-morning assembly line, there was little choice. Accordingly the bakeries became magnets for factory workers, cops, cabbies, truck drivers, and the rest of America's working class. In many ways the shops replaced the urban diners and coffee shops that had thrived before the war. There was the same sort of neighborhood feeling, the conversation, the sense that you were a regular. Fast-food chains like McDonald's and Burger King served you at a window and sent you on your way, whereas the counters typical of many early donut shops gave you time and space to linger. There were the girls too. As in the trenches of the Western Front, the predominantly male, early-morning clientele got its coffee and sinkers from young women. Here, again, the contrast with the burger chains couldn't have been starker: where McDonald's and its imitators specifically had a policy to discourage female counter workers so as to limit fraternization (Ray Crock, the burger chain's founder, originally banned all women workers because they "attracted the wrong kind of boys"), donut shops typically had the opposite policy. While the donut bakers in the back were most likely male, the front counter was invariably staffed by women.

Naturally, donut shops weren't just patronized by Homer Simpson and his kind. At certain times of day the clientele was more varied. When Canadian donut scholar Steve Penfold interviewed shop owners and workers, they often spoke of a predictable rhythm to the day. The truck drivers came in first thing, then the salesmen; housewives doing shopping stopped by in the afternoon; while in the evening, the shops were hangouts for teenagers; bar patrons came in after midnight, and the cabbies after that. Some of the customers were rich, a few were poor, but most were in the middle. A 1959 study found that middle-income families bought 62 percent more donuts than those at either end of the economic scale. Admittedly many blue-collar workers, whether cops or factory workers, considered themselves squarely in the middle class.

The donut shops knew full well they couldn't just depend on shift workers to pay the bills, so they looked for locations in shopping malls and middle-income neighborhoods, and advertised to baby boomers' parents with their rapidly multiplying, donut-hungry offspring. They also made sure to make their shops safe and wholesome, and to this end they did everything to attract another kind of customer: the policeman.

## COPS AND DONUTS

So what is it about cops and donuts? In line at Brooklyn's Peter Pan donut shop the other day, I asked one of a half dozen cops standing in front of me about the connection. The strapping African American officer gave me the sort of look a Great Dane would give a yappy Chihuahua and assured me that it was just one of those clichés. "We come here because the donuts are really good here," he explained. It may be a generational thing. When I called up Lou Clark, a family friend and a twenty-five-year veteran of the Oakland Police Department, he was full of cop and donut lore. It may well be that today, the fried pastry's connection to the law is no more than an urban legend, but it was sure as hell alive and well in California in the early sixties. "In those days," Lou told me, "when cops lined up for their morning inspections with spots on their uniforms, their superiors would play guessing games as to the flavor of donut that caused the stains." Overweight cops were ribbed for their donut addiction. When bulky bulletproof vests were introduced around 1963, people joked that the cops looked like they'd spent the last month in a donut shop.

Like many clichés, the bond between police officers and fried dough has a backstory. Imagine yourself in a police cruiser patrolling the asphalt jungle of the naked city. It's four in the morning, and you need some sugar and a cup of Joe to make it through your shift. Where do you go? There's nothing open except the donut joint. Norm Stamper, the former chief of the Seattle Police Department, points out how barren the grazing grounds were in the early days of the patrol car. "When it came to Code 7 (meal break), graveyard cops in the forties and fifties had few choices," he writes. "They could pack lunch, pray for an all night diner on their beat, or fill up on doughnuts. Doughnuts usually won out. They were, to most palates, tasty,

Whether myth or reality, cops are inescapably linked to donuts in the American imagination.

and they were cheap and convenient." Frank Rizzo, the straight-shooting former mayor and police chief of Philadelphia, recalled his early years at the department in the late 1940s, when cops ate donuts and got respect. "Let me tell you that when I was cop—even though I had my breakfast at home—there was nothing I liked more than *a big, thick doughnut and a cup of coffee!* You got out there, walked around, rolled in the streets with criminals [and burned] the calories off." By the mid-sixties there were other options, but donuts still retained an attraction for beat cops. Dick Ellwood, in a memoir of his time on the Baltimore police force, recalls the allure of the bakery in the wee hours of the morning. "I can remember standing on that corner [near Lindingers Bakery] when I worked the midnight shift and the bakers would come to work about 4 AM and start to make the cakes and doughnuts for the day," he writes of his rookie days in the 1960s. "I would work my way to the front of the window and wave to the bakers, knowing they would invite me in, especially when it was cold. . . . I would eat a few doughnuts right off the assembly line and they were hot and some of them you did not even have to chew, they just slid down your throat." In Oakland, Lou Clark explained, the donut bakers had every incentive to keep the officers hanging around: "The owners liked the police car parked out there because that way the bad guys wouldn't come around." William Rosenberg, the founder of Dunkin' Donuts, had an explicit policy of making his stores "hospitable" to the police. "This attitude served our company well," he notes in his autobiography, "it protected the stores and it kept the crime rate very low." How many officers actually paid for their sinkers and java is an open question. Manuals on police ethics typically list coffee and donuts as one of the most common "gratuities" offered to policemen. The professional journal *Police* spells it out as early as 1964: "Do not accept gifts—donuts and coffee. This gives the impression of partiality." Well that was the whole point, wasn't it?

*THE DONUT*

Yet my Peter Pan donut shop informant was probably right, the days of cops and donuts may now be as dated as *Dragnet* and *Columbo*. As far back as 1991, cheeky *Spy* magazine staked out a half dozen donut shops—each near a precinct house during the prime donut hours of 6:45 and 8:45 AM—yet all the journalistic SWAT team could uncover was a single perp—just one police officer ordering a solitary sinker. The intrepid reporters subsequently collared the NYPD's spokesperson, but he confessed to eating bran muffins for breakfast. Finally, when the newshounds called in the executive director of the National Association of Chiefs of Police as an expert witness, his first instinct was to cast doubt on the investigators' findings by citing the following donut-eating metrics: "I would say that on a scale of 1 to 10, [cops] probably rank somewhere around a 10½." Nonetheless, under cross-examination he admitted that he too had lapsed in his donut habit, copping a plea that his diabetes should be submitted as an extenuating circumstance. What's next? Police officers filling up on decaf chai lattes? If nothing else, at least the legend of the cop and the donut lives on, even if only in the form of a punch line.

## FUNNY DONUT

It's a documented fact that donuts are funny. Just ask America's favorite fictional everyman, Homer Simpson. Or in my case, I did the next best thing: I asked someone who has been an intimate acquaintance of the yellow-skinned, donut-dreaming celebrity from day one, the executive producer of *The Simpsons*, Al Jean. So why are donuts funny? "Well just look at the words: 'dough' and 'nut.' They're both hilarious!" he told me. Pondering the question for another millisecond, Jean added, "It's dough with a hole in the middle for no reason," as if it were just begging for ridicule. For the purposes of a cartoon, the distinctive shape has other uses: it makes the pastries recognizable whether they're hot pink or the size of a UFO.

The creators of *The Simpsons* were hardly the first to yuk it up with fried dough. As early as 1883, Jessup Whitehead asks rhetorically, "Why does everybody laugh when there are doughnuts in the case? Yet they did. In a widely reprinted love letter supposedly penned by a besotted Southerner some fifteen years earlier (to the victors of the Civil War, Southerners were almost as funny then as cartoon nuclear plant workers are today), the author declares his sweetheart "fairer than a speckled pullet, sweeter than a Yankee dough-nut fried in sorghum

## DONUT SLANG

**Surfin' USA:**
*donut:* The inside of a round hollow wave

**Spin City:**
*donut:* to make a car spin by pulling up on the hand brake

**Sinker IQ:**
*donut head:* used as a term of abuse suggesting an empty head

**Peewee League Thug:**
*coffee-and-donut gun:* a second-rate, unthreatening gangster (1920s)

**Nerd About Town:**
*donut hole:* a person with no social skills

**Sure Thing:**
*dollars to donuts:* denoting a high level of certainty

molasses, brighter than the top knot plumage on the head of a Muscovy duck." OK, our idea of humor has changed—but more in style than substance. Decades later the donut was still the "buffoon of the bakery," as *Printer's Ink* called it in 1920, and continued to be the butt of jokes and a "perennial source of levity…forever cast as the comedian of the breakfast table."

And not just breakfast; the donut also played it for laughs on stage and screen. In the 1904 "The Great Doughnut Corporation," the donut was the leading player in the one-act play about a fried dough Ponzi scheme. In *Angora Love,* Laurel and Hardy's last silent movie, a goat and a donut deserved equal billing with the famous comics. The plot—subtitled "The dramatic story of a goat"—opens with the escape of Penelope the goat from a pet store. Soon after, we spot the two slapstick virtuosos exiting a confectionary shop with a bag of sinkers in hand. "You'd spend our last dime for pastry with a hole in it!" quips Ollie to his pal even as Penelope wanders into the frame. The bearded ingénue clearly shares Stan's holey pastry predilection, because once he gives her a taste, she gloms onto the comedic duo for the movie's remaining twenty minutes of mayhem.

In 1933, Shirley Temple played along a cast of sinkers in *Dora's Dunking Doughnuts,* a short, goofy movie about a donut shop. Donuts get a cameo in the 1938 romantic comedy *Having a Wonderful Time* and a role in Busby Berkeley's extravagantly silly *The Gang's All Here*

(1943). Perhaps the best-known specimen of donut cinematography is the 1963 film *Dough-nuts*, an adaptation of a Robert McCloskey story featuring Homer Price and an unstoppable automatic donut machine. The precocious Homer gets himself in a jam with his uncle's brand-new machine. Not only is it missing some essential parts that won't let it stop, but when he overloads it with batter, a diamond bracelet ends up getting lost in its gears. A few thousand sinkers later, Homer comes up with a contest to find the diamond-filled donut, and our hero can move on to other misadventures.

Donuts weren't merely funny; they could be sappy, silly, and sophomoric too. And not only were they featured in movies, there is also an extensive donut discography. A quick troll of iTunes in 2013 yielded a cache of some two thousand songs, artists, or albums with *donut* (or *doughnut*) in their name. The Christian children's troubadour, the Donut Man, adapted his name from one of his early, inimitable lyrics, "Life without Jesus is like a donut; there's a hole in the middle of your heart." The Donuts are a rock quartet. Bag of Donuts sings pop, and Alice Donut is a punk band from New York City. In songs, sinkers show up on the road, in hard-core clubs, and in the ghetto. In the Mills Brothers' "A Donut and a Dream," the pop quartet tell a sentimental story of a lonesome drifter sick of one-night stands with waitresses on the road. In a more practical vein, the nineties L.A. punk band NOFX composed the rant "Cops and Donuts," a how-to guide to evading traffic tickets by greasing police officers' palms with jelly donuts. In the 1992 hip-hop hit, "A Day of Sooperman Lover," rapper Red-man is rewarded with coffee and donuts (also jelly) by a grateful "badass dame" for finding her cat—or at least that's the G-rated part of her gratitude.

Needless to say, donuts have meant many things to many people. For New Englanders, they were a badge of identity in the young republic; for Yankee sailors, they were a taste of home; for GIs in both World Wars, they symbolized what they were fighting for. By the mid-twentieth century, donuts were as American as—well, you get the idea. To some they were a sign of courage, to others a lard-laced punch line. The sage of Springfield hit it right on the head when he mused, "Donuts, is there anything they can't do?"

Today, nobody thinks of motherhood and country when they bite into an old-fashioned. The donut is more American than ever, but in a way that brings to mind Dunkin' Donuts and Coke rather than Mom and apple pie. For better or worse, donuts are ubiquitous.

# 4

# DONUTS HIGH
# AND LOW

The United States was changing. In the late eighteen hundreds, factories had begun to smother the countryside even as the cities were engorged with arrivals from rural America and Europe alike. It was an era of speeding locomotives, electric lights, and virtually instant communication courtesy of the telegraph. Increasingly, everyone was in a hurry. Certainly a modern American had no time for a leisurely morning meal. As a consequence, breakfast cereals—formerly a food restricted to crackpots and invalids—became a runaway success, perfect for typists or factory workers rushing to their morning jobs. Better yet was the coffee and donut you could consume at a corner coffee shop before hopping on the streetcar or bus. But there was a problem with donuts. In an age of hand rolling and cutting, the pastries were laborious to make, and professional bakers found the hot oil a hassle. The solution, in this technology-besotted age, was there for anyone to see: automation. Henry Ford had done it with the Model T; Milton Hershey for the Hershey Bar. So why not the donut?

This idea first occurred to a group of Washington businessmen in 1919, leading them to found the Square Donut Company of America. Like others of their generation, they had noticed the newfound popularity of the fried pastry among returning doughboys. Trying to come up with a new angle on the round donut, they came upon the notion of squaring the circle. The result? "*A patented machine* which produces *square donuts* faster and more *economically* than doughnuts were ever manufactured before," as the following year's stock offering put it.

Presumably, if the donuts were rectilinear, you could easily package them and the novelty would make marketing a cinch. The first ads for Dono, "The Square Meal Square Donuts," appeared on streetcars in time for New Year's Day 1920. Newspaper ads informed readers that it was "just the thing for the school luncheon—the business luncheon—or the home luncheon. An appetizing bite for any time you would tantalize the appetite." Alas the business plan didn't quite turn out as anticipated. Perhaps the Washington investors underestimated the difficulties of fitting a square peg into a round hole or maybe their pastries weren't just the thing for businessmen's luncheons or any other meal. Or maybe they just weren't any good. Nevertheless, even if the Dono never managed to tantalize anyone's appetite, the fundamental idea of industrializing donut production wasn't merely a crackpot idea concocted to fleece unsuspecting investors. The concept was sound; it's just that the donuts had to taste good too.

## THE DOUGHNUT CORPORATION OF AMERICA

In the end, it was a Russian Jewish immigrant who would usher in the donut automation revolution. Adolph Levitt was an eight-year-old village boy when he and his family of eight joined his older brother in Milwaukee in 1892. According to his granddaughter Sally Levitt Steinberg, who recounted the family saga in *The Donut Book: The Whole Story in Words, Pictures & Outrageous Tales*, the young Adolph had to quit school at ten in order to help support the family, which he did by peddling the daily paper to local brothels. Presumably having learned something about men's needs as well as underwear, he went into the haberdasher business with his brothers, sequentially opening and—it seems—soon closing stores across the Midwest.

By the time he was thirty-seven, he was broke and ready to get out of town. Lucky for Adolph, he had a Jewish mother. Who but a doting Jewish mother would trust her savings to a sequential business failure with yet another harebrained business scheme? And in New York no less? But her devotion was rewarded. Years later she could boast about her son, the donut millionaire. What Levitt did with his mother's savings was move to Harlem and buy into a local bakery chain. It was now 1920, and the all-American donut was riding its postwar wave of popularity. Like the Washington donut investors a year earlier, Levitt saw the opportunity. But how to take advantage of it?

One thing that the future donut mogul seemed to have learned from his previous ventures is that if you want to attract customers, you need to put your best goods where people can see them. With that in mind he set up a kettle of grease in the window of his Harlem bakery and fried his pastries in full view of the passing pedestrians. The gimmick worked so well that he couldn't keep up with his clamoring customers. If only he could automate the process, do for the donut what Ford had done for the automobile, he could satisfy his hungry clientele and make his mother proud. But Levitt did not have the tinkering skill of a Henry Ford. The concept of bringing the greasy, dangerous donut-making process into the machine age became reality only though sheer serendipity, when Levitt happened to meet an engineer on a train ride to Chicago. A dozen prototypes later, they had themselves a contraption that cranked out dough rings automatically and then flipped them halfway through frying. It was a thing of beauty.

Almost as soon as he had a working prototype, he set up the Display Doughnut Machine Corporation (later the Doughnut Corporation of America) to sell it to independent bakeries. The machines were a huge hit with bakers, who ordered 128 of the devices in the first year alone. But it wasn't just the pros who were enamored of the donut gizmo. In 1931, James Thurber became enraptured by one of the "Wonderful Almost Human Automatic Donut Machines," as they were called, when he stumbled upon it in Times Square. "Doughnuts float dreamily through a grease canal in a glass-enclosed machine," Thurber wrote in the *New Yorker*, "walk dreamily up a moving ramp, and tumble dreamily into an outgoing basket."

To keep the dream alive for all his bakery customers, Levitt created a standardized mix that needed little more than water. He also supplied his industry customers with optional trade names: Downyflake and Mayflower were the best known. This was the mix used by the Red Cross "we weigh the water" volunteers in the Second World War and by untold numbers of donut bakers across the United States and eventually Canada, England, and Australia too. Yet even that wasn't the culmination of Levitt's donut ambition. In 1949, the Corporation opened up a five-story laboratory dedicated to an "elaborate apparatus that tests every step in the making of this once lowly fried cake," as the *New York Times* put it. By this point Levitt's organization was the largest maker of donut mixes in the world. "In the early days," wrote one industry watcher in 1948, "a qualified baker could cut and fry something like 250 dozen daily," while Levitt's first machine could manufacture eighty dozen *per hour*. Now, the number had risen to six hundred dozen per hour.

Levitt didn't merely run the wholesale operation though. He took what he'd learned in Harlem and turned it into a chain of donut restaurants, the Mayflower Shops. He opened branches in Miami and Minneapolis, in Boston and L.A., each emblazoned with the dunker's motto "As you ramble through life, keep your eye on the doughnut and not on the hole."

It wasn't Levitt's technical wizardry that ultimately made the company prosper and grow, but rather his magic touch for PR. In 1928, he dreamed up October as National Doughnut Month as a run-up to Halloween at a time when donuts were considered an indispensable treat for trick-or-treating goblins and ghouls. As if that wasn't

Vaudeville Stars Willie and Eugene Howard dunk at the 1939 World's Fair.

enough, 1935 saw the birth of National Doughnut Week. The following year, he employed a New York ad agency to coordinate the sale of Mayflower donuts in hundreds of bakeries nationwide, giving rise to the first nationally branded donut. Then in 1939, he followed through with what *Time* magazine described as the "screwiest publicity campaigns in advertising history." At the opening of the World's Fair, the Doughnut Corporation of America set up two exhibits decorated with murals telling the story of the donut. The showrooms were so large that up to fourteen hundred donut "dunkers" could be accommodated at one time.

Even as the parent company itself kept an almost anonymous profile, it invented the National Dunking Association in 1939 and successfully wooed actors, athletes, congressmen, and other celebrities to sign on. At one time, Zero Mostel, Johnny Carson, and even the modern dance virtuoso Martha Graham were card-carrying dunkers. In the 1940s, the organization boasted three million members. They somehow even convinced the famed novelist Pearl Buck to get up onstage and declare that world peace could be achieved if only people started dunking. "If Mayor LaGuardia and Hitler only would get together," the Nobel

Across the country, the American Doughnut Corporation of America helped organize beauty contests to promote their all-American pastry.

Prize winner explained, "and dunk a couple of doughnuts, they would see life through the same rose-colored glasses." Topping the ridiculous with the absurd, the dunking fad hit its apogee when celebrity flagpole sitter Alvin "Shipwreck" Kelly stood on his head atop Manhattan's fifty-six-story-high Chanin Building, where he ate thirteen doughnuts one Friday the Thirteenth.

By 1940, the Doughnut Corporation of America had a virtual monopoly on the American industry. A year earlier, US donut sales were estimated at some $78 million, or the equivalent of about four billion sinkers. Eighty percent of those were made on the donut behemoth's machines and more than 30 percent were from the company's own mix. *Time* pronounced Levitt "boss of the doughnut world." He preferred "the Donut King."

Despite its dominance, the New York donut giant didn't entirely have the market to itself. Belshaw Brothers, founded in Seattle in 1923, may not have been the first to automate the donut-making process, but the scrappy company is one of the only pioneers still in business. Today, they make automated machines huge and small. In Seattle's Pike Place Market, a tiny donut stand called Daily Dozen sells the freshest donuts you may ever buy. They drop down in a continuous stream from a Belshaw model little bigger than a toaster oven. They're hot, greasy, and addictive. At the other end of the scale, Belshaw counts the US Navy as a client—one of their automated donut contraptions was installed on the aircraft carrier USS *Enterprise*. Their machines also spew out sinkers in prisons from San Quentin, California, to Atlanta, Georgia. This does present some challenges apparently; according to Mike Baxter, Belshaw's marketing director, "They use a special prison package machine, one that can't be easily disassembled to make shivs." Yet compared to the leviathans

Many of the early donut machines were operated by hand like this 1923 model from Belshaw.

# ON DUNKING

People have undoubtedly been dunking donuts ever since there were donuts and something to dunk them in. Let's face it, after a couple of days, what else are you going to do with the thing? Dipping the stale pastry into hot liquid makes it almost palatable again. And in the days of wooden teeth, chewable too. That said, who would expect dunking to turn into a fad that would take the country by storm in the 1940s? Legend has it that dunking first took off when silent movie sensation Mae Murray dipped her donut in public, something considered quite déclassé at the time. More likely the beginning of the craze could be traced to a gag routine the popular comic Richard "Red" Skelton had developed for the stage (and later screen)—as well as with a helping hand from the Doughnut Corporation of America.

Skelton apparently developed the skit during a vaudeville run in Montreal in 1938, where it became the hit of his act. Here too, the premise was that it was impolite to dunk in public, so Skelton went through a battery of gags so that he wouldn't be caught red-handed; of course he always was. The comic ended up doing three shows a day, eating a dozen sinkers each time. He apparently gained thirty-five pounds but also the attention of Hollywood, who drafted him to do the routine in a Ginger Rogers film, *Having a Wonderful Time*. The recently organized Dunkers Association took note too, made him its titular president, and promptly plastered his image on restaurant displays. Dunking, long the scourge of polite society, became not only OK but de rigueur. In 1947, in observance of National Donut Week, the National Dunking Association issued advice on the proper scientific approach to the matter. "Dunking the complete donut is regarded as crude and inefficient," the report noted, "the donut should be broken in half before dunking. The half should be dunked long enough to absorb the full flavor of the liquid, but not so long as to get soggy; the proper timing is two and one-half seconds. Beginners are advised to tie napkins under their chins." Just in case you were wondering.

that dominate the world donut market, the Seattle manufacturer is a minnow. That may have been to its advantage though. It's too small a morsel for the world's hungry multinationals to bother with.

It has been a different story with the Doughnut Corporation of America. In a rapidly globalizing economy, it was just too tempting a dish to pass up. In 1972, two decades after Levitt's passing, it was swallowed by the UK-based company Lyons. Some years later, the same British-based conglomerate (now called Allied Lyons) would absorb Dunkin' Donuts too. That meant that it was now a European multinational that could claim the title of the world's undisputed donut boss.

## DUNKIN' DONUTS

The story of Dunkin' Donuts has more than one similarity to the rags-to-riches tale of the Doughnut Corporation of America. Like Levitt, Dunkin' Donuts' founder, William Rosenberg, was a Jewish boy who grew up poor and hungry for success. Born in 1916, Rosenberg was raised in a working-class neighborhood in Boston, the son of a struggling grocer. Years later, he remembered how he was initiated into the New England donut cult. As he tells it, the five-year-old future tycoon and his older sister would bundle up into Pop Rosenberg's Model T truck at five in the morning to pick up supplies for the store at the wholesale market in Faneuil Hall. The highlight of the trip was the diner, located in the center of the rowdy sales floor. "That's where they sold the biggest nickel jelly donuts you ever saw," Rosenberg writes in his autobiography, *Time to Make the Donuts*. "Boy, those big jelly donuts, yeast raised with granulated sugar on the outside, were so loaded with jelly that when we took a bite out of one, it would squirt. It was fantastic!"

It would take many years before little Billy's enthusiasm would translate into the world's greatest donut empire. In the interim, he had to live with the consequences of his father's inept business decisions and the Great Depression. The young Rosenberg dropped out of school after eighth grade to take a job as a Western Union delivery boy. But there wasn't much money or glamour in that. For an urban kid, the dream job was driving an ice cream truck. You could drive a shiny white truck, dress in a snazzy all-white uniform, and go where you pleased. As soon as he could get a driver's license, the seventeen-year-old dropout got the job. He was a natural salesman and quickly turned the second-rate routes he was assigned into some of the most profitable. The ice cream company owners took note. Five years on, the kid from the wrong side of the tracks was head manager for Jack and Jill's ice cream operation in New Haven, Connecticut. When the Second World War came, he found work in a factory deemed necessary for the war effort. The factory job proved a revelation. As soon as the conflict ended, Rosenberg set out on his own, setting up a business that catered to the same blue-collar workers he had come to know on the shop floor. His company, Industrial Luncheon Service, would pull up trucks in front of factories, offering fresh coffee, sandwiches, and baked goods for the workers to buy during their breaks. Later, the catering company got contracts to run cafeterias too.

As Rosenberg's organization grew, he came to realize that more and more of his business comprised coffee and donuts, some 40 percent by his estimate. But it took a conversation with an alcoholic Swede before he put two and two together. The eureka moment came as he was getting ready to fire his donut baker, Alvin Johnson. As Rosenberg tells it, the besotted Scandinavian was telling his boss about the retail donut operation of his previous employer. "Do you know someting, Bill?" he began, "Ve had twelve wholesale trucks, and vhen ve opened a liddle retail store in front of de donut-making plant, ve made more money from dat one store den ve made from de twelve wholesale trucks."

The lightbulb lit up above Rosenberg's head as he considered the potential and began to tick off all the advantages. Once you remove the delivery expenses, the remaining costs are trivial. After all, you're dealing with a product that's little more than sugar, flour, and fat. And what about those other donut shops? The Doughnut Corporation's Mayflower Shops "were going along pretty good," Rosenberg thought to himself. Then he remembered Freddie's Donuts, a place he'd visited in Buffalo, New York, that always seemed mobbed, and Cottage Donuts, which already had two successful branches in the greater Boston area. Why not give it a shot? Alvin got to keep his job, at least for now.

The first Dunkin' Donuts branch was in the unassuming Boston suburb of Quincy.

His partner, Harry Winokur, wasn't as enthusiastic, but with a little targeted cajoling and a pointed threat or two, Rosenberg eventually convinced him to support the donut shop. The grand opening came on Memorial Day 1950. They built the first branch in Quincy, just outside Boston, naming it Open Kettle to give it that old-fashioned New England ring. And what of Alvin, the inspiration of Rosenberg's empire of dough? Alas, the baker didn't prove to have

Coffee as much as donuts were the foundation of Bill Rosenberg's (pictured) fried dough empire.

the longevity of the donut shop. One day he just disappeared, without even leaving behind a track of crumbs.

The Quincy store took a somewhat different tack than most donut retail stores, which were little more than shop fronts. Perhaps taking a cue from the Mayflower chain, Rosenberg put in seats and added coffee, tea, milk, and hot chocolate to the menu so the customers would have a reason to linger. He knew full well from his catering business that there was more money in coffee than in food. Yet when it came to the fry cakes themselves, there, too, he thought outside of the box. Typical donut bakeries had only four kinds of donuts: plain cake, jelly, yeast-raised, and a cruller. Rosenberg wondered, if the neighboring Howard Johnson (also first opened in Quincy) could sell twenty-eight varieties of ice cream, why couldn't his new shop offer just as many kinds of donuts, or even more? Consequently, the shop experimented with a new flavor each week. (Today, Dunkin' Donuts offers more than seventy varieties of donuts.) At five cents a donut and ten cents for a cup of coffee, the new business pulled in as much as $5,500 a week. That was almost double what most Boston families took home in a year!

Sales were doing well but Rosenberg didn't much like the name, so, about a year and a half after Open Kettle's premiere, he convened a brainstorming session with his staff. Someone suggested "Mister Donut." Another employee came up with "Best Donuts"; then Bernard Healy, the store's recently hired architect, mumbled, "What the hell do you do with a donut? You pick a chicken, you pluck a chicken, you dunk a donut..."

"That's it!" Rosenberg yelled out and that was that. Soon enough they pulled down the Open Kettle sign to replace it with DUNKIN' DONUTS, THE WORLD'S FINEST COFFEE.

Like Levitt, Rosenberg understood that a little theater could help keep the patrons piling in. Accordingly, many of the early branches had a window that looked into the production room so that the customers could watch the bakers roll out the dough, dust it, cut the donuts, put them on a screen, and fry them. The clientele loved it and kept coming back for more.

By 1955, the company started franchising, but you couldn't just plop down a Dunkin' Donuts any old place. In order to find the best spots, headquarters figured out a multipoint system to identify potential locations. For example, they looked around for kids' bikes in surrounding neighborhoods, figuring that children ate more donuts than adults did. That same year the simmering tension between Rosenberg and his partner, Harry Winokur, came to a head. The breakup wasn't entirely amicable, and Winokur set up a competing chain, snatching the name Mister Donut for his own fried dough kingdom.

By 1963, there were a hundred Dunkin' Donut stores; in 1979 there were a thousand. In the meantime, the company had gone public. Then in 1989, just about the time when its two thousandth branch was about to open, Dunkin' Donuts was bought out by the same British company that had gobbled up the Doughnut Corporation of America. The following year, a similar fate befell Harry Winokur's Mister Donut, or at least its American operations. If anything, this consolidation only accelerated Dunkin's conquest of the world: most of the Mister Donuts were repainted pink and orange, and, as of 2013, there were more than ten thousand Dunkin' Donuts restaurants in thirty-one countries.

Other donut chains have had more modest success. On the West Coast, Winchell's opened its roadside donut operation in 1948, growing to over 170 branches in the subsequent sixty years. In the South, Krispy Kreme has been producing its signature sinkers since 1937. However the place where the donut chain would find the most fertile ground wasn't in the United States at all but rather in the frigid backyard of its next-door neighbor.

## DONUTS, EH?

Tim Horton grew up some 250 miles north of the US border, where he learned to play hockey on a frozen lake. He was a good-looking kid in a hunky, farm boy kind of way. He was also a whiz with the puck, which eventually landed him his dream job as a hockey player with the Toronto Maple Leafs. Still, while hockey may be Canada's national religion, its practitioners haven't always been well rewarded. In the early 1950s, when Horton was drafted by the Leafs franchise, he made so little money that he would spend summers back home lugging beer for the Provincial beer company. Looking for an alternative source of income, he

## PINK AND ORANGE

Life is full of kooky coincidences. In my case, I happen to be married to the woman whose childhood preferences determined the Dunkin' Donuts color scheme. Back in the early 1970s, her industrial designer mom, Lucia N. DeRespinis, was working on the prototype of a new Dunkin' Donuts interior. There was to be a beige-and-orange interior as well as donut-shaped light fixtures. The graphic designers had, in the meantime, come up with a variety of typeface options, all of which hewed to a beige-and-brown color palette. Poking her nose into the graphics department, DeRespinis wondered aloud why everything was brown.

"Well, it's about donuts," the graphic designer replied.

"That hotdog typeface is great but why not a color?"

"It's donuts."

"Why not make that hotdog typeface orange and pink?" DeRespinis persisted. "Orange and pink are my daughter's favorite colors. Every birthday party I have ever had for her is ALL orange and pink."

Forty years later, both my mother-in-law and her pink-and-orange donut logo are going strong.

opened a hamburger stand in the 1950s and even owned a gas station and a Studebaker dealership a decade later. But of course that isn't why Tim Horton is a household name north of the forty-ninth parallel, nor is his distinguished hockey career—though that doesn't hurt. In Canada, Tim Hortons is as much a part of the national identity as McDonald's and Coke are across the border. Dunkin' Donuts is just a donut chain; "Timmies" is Valhalla.

According to Lori Horton, Tim's widow (the hockey star died in a drunk driving accident in 1974), her husband was a "confirmed donut fanatic from way back." When he and Lori drove down to see her family in Pittsburgh, he would often go out of his way to stop at a little donut shop in Erie, Pennsylvania, to get a dozen or two for the road. Nonetheless, he more or less stumbled into the donut business when he met and befriended Jim Charade in 1963. The two made a bit of a Felix-and-Oscar combination. The French Canadian Charade was an aspiring R&B drummer and dressed the part in silk suits and loud ties, whereas Horton was almost the cliché of a good-hearted hick. What may have brought them together was that for both of them, the donuts were just the day job. Charade had worked for Vachon, a large wholesale bakery, and had also opened up a small chain of donut shops on his own, so he knew something about fried dough. He figured with his experience and Horton's fame, they could make a go of it. Ironically, though, the hockey star wasn't initially interested in donuts. What he wanted was to open more burger joints, which he did, and which failed one after another.

It wasn't until 1964 that he and Charade opened up the first Tim Horton donuts (the original lacked the "s") in the blue-collar town of Hamilton, Ontario. An early box design featured the hockey player's autograph and an image of four donuts, one for each of his daughters. Unfortunately, Horton's luck with the puck didn't always transfer to his business

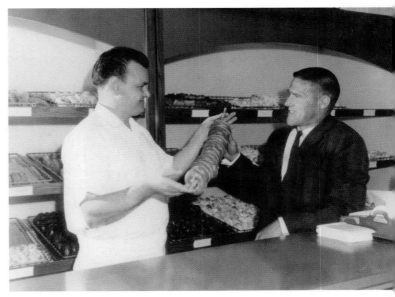

Tim Horton (on the right) and Ron Joyce in the early days.

ventures, and it didn't help matters that Jim Charade lived up to his surname when it came to keeping the books. The donut business almost went bust until Ron Joyce, a veteran of the Hamilton Police Department and the Dairy Queen Corporation, bought into it in 1966. Well if there's one thing cops knew back then, it was donuts. With Joyce at the helm, just five years later there were thirty stores. By the early nineties there were more than eight hundred, and today, Tim Hortons has over three thousand stores in Canada alone. That works out to roughly four times as many Timmies per capita as there are Dunkin' Donuts per capita in the United States. It's widely reported that Canadians top the world in per-person donut consumption, though tracking down the actual statistics is about as easy as spotting a polar bear in a Yukon snowstorm.

The exact reasons for the northern donut obsession are a little hard to pin down. After all, donuts are an American import, yet somehow, associating them with hockey has allowed Canadians to make the fried dough rings their own. Presumably the cold has something to do with the popularity of both. Steve Penfold, the Canadian donut scholar, thinks that it has

## ASIAN INVASION

No one has embraced the all-American donut with greater enthusiasm than East Asians. Whereas in the United States, Mister Donut is more or less kaput, it has over ten thousand shops throughout Japan, the Philippines, Thailand, and other Asian locations, easily beating Dunkin' Donuts at its game. And as far as innovation goes, these shops are leaving their American cousins in the dust. Among the most popular recent inventions are the chewy *pon-de-rings*, which take the shape of oversized pearl bracelets. These come in flavors such as cherry blossom, green tea, and bean paste, and are glazed in colors that look like they're on loan from Fisher Price. But even regular donuts have gotten a makeover. Would you believe wasabi cheese or seaweed cheese donuts? Or fried pork–dusted donuts? Or kimchi-filled donuts? All seen, respectively, at Dunkin' Donuts in Singapore, China, and Korea. Try topping *that*, Brooklyn hipster donut dudes!

something to do with the national sense of irony that occasionally sweeps south (think Mike Myers or Jim Carrey), much like those Arctic cold fronts. One way that Canadians try to distinguish themselves from their southern neighbor is through a kind of self-consciousness about anything perceived as American. It's as if they were playing dress-up. According to this theory, the donut and the donut shop were the perfect ironic foil through which Canadians could both recognize and separate themselves from the dominating American culture. Sounds like a lot to ask of a lump of dough, doesn't it? It may be more straightforward than that. The unpretentious, unglamorous, and thoroughly egalitarian donut echoes all those same qualities that Canadians see and admire in themselves. It also happens to be cold outside, and there's nothing quite like a warm donut and a hot cup of coffee on an ice-bound Canadian winter day. But whatever the reason—whether it's because of their deep cultural significance or pure happenstance—donuts have become as much a part of Canadian identity as hockey, beer, and Celine Dion. Which is all well and good, though as William Shatner, Justin Bieber, and other famous Canadians will tell you, the real test is success down south.

In 2009, on a steamy summer Friday night in July, a dozen New York City Dunkin' Donuts closed up shop. Teams of construction workers moved in and ripped out the pink-and-orange signs, the menu boards with their French crullers, Boston kremes, glazed old-fashioneds, and strawberry Coolattas. The transformation was engineered by Gary Trimarchi, a big-time Dunkin' Donut franchisee who had gone sour on the brand. In looking for a replacement, he stumbled across Timmies' slick operation up north. It helped that Trimarchi was a hockey fan, so the Horton name actually meant something to the Queens native. It took the whole dusty weekend, but come Monday, New Yorkers awoke to a new kid in town: the old donut shops were reborn as Tim Hortons. From the trendy Lower East Side to the tony Upper East Side to Madison Square Garden, where Tim had once played for the Rangers, the Canadian invader threw down the gauntlet.

Whether anybody in New York actually noticed is another matter. "Hortons, shmortons…" wrote the inimitable wordsmiths at the *New York Post*. The *Times* was noncommittal. These weren't the only outposts south of the border. As of 2012, Tim Hortons had opened over seven hundred branches in the United States, but they have typically averaged half the sales of Canadian stores. In New York, the locals are a fickle lot. A decade earlier they'd fallen in love with another beloved donut chain, only to dump it for the next fresh floozy to come along.

## *KRISPY KREME*

Where the Tim Hortons 2009 New York debut made barely a ripple, Krispy Kreme's earlier coming-out party made a splash that poured down a monsoon's worth of hype. When the North Carolina–based donut chain opened its first New York branch on West 23rd Street in 1996, the Southern humorist Roy Blount Jr. wrote a paean to the risen dough ring that would get a PR copywriter fired for the purpleness of his prose. "When Krispy Kremes are hot, they are to other doughnuts what angels are to people," the usually acerbic Blount wrote in the *New York Times*. "Kind of like fried nectar puffed up with yeast." Not to be outdone, the *New Yorker* sent the writer and movie director Nora Ephron to report on the Krispy Kreme donut craze sweeping the Big Apple. Like Blount, she was transfigured by the experience. "The modest, clean Krispy Kreme doughnut store…has become a shrine," she wrote, adding, "the sort of religious experience New Yorkers like me are far more receptive to than ones that actually involve God."

Like other donut chains, Krispy Kreme franchises took part in the growing suburbanization of America.

The Krispy Kreme cult had been introduced to Sodom on the Hudson by Mel Lev, a shirt manufacturer who had experienced *his* conversion in Jackson, Mississippi. While Lev was staying at a local hotel, a friend had introduced him to the Southern icon and, after apparently imbibing four sinkers in the backseat of a car, the New Yorker saw the light. And as Ephron noted, godless Manhattanites flocked to his temple of fried dough—at least for a time.

Krispy Kreme is easily the oldest of today's large donut chains and certainly elicits the most devotion among its customers. The company likes to play up its Southern roots. According to the officially sanctioned legend, the top-secret recipe and name both harken back to a donut shop in Paducah, Kentucky, purportedly owned by Joe LeBeau, a French chef from New Orleans. He was alleged to have sold the shop and recipe to Ishmael Armstrong in 1933, who, in turn, taught the formula to his eighteen-year-old nephew Vernon Rudolph, who then went on to found the company we know today.

While the Rudolf part of the story seems likely enough, the origin story may be more tangled than Krispy Kreme's promotional literature lets on. For one, the LeBeau connection looks like it's hokum. When, in the 1980s, one of the company's lawyers went down to Paducah to investigate the story, he could find no trace of a Joe LeBeau. In 1997, curious about the discrepancy, Carver Rudolph, the founder's son, enlisted a local Kentucky historian to look into the matter. He too could find no mention of any Joe LeBeau or even a donut shop in 1933. His research did, however, identify a Joseph G. LeBoeuf who had once worked as a cook on a barge on the Ohio and was once famous for his light and fluffy donuts. But there seemed to be no indication of any financial transaction or a secret recipe. As best as the historian and Rudolph fils were able to figure out, that original recipe consisted of a "cream" (thus the name) of beaten egg whites, mashed potatoes, sugar, shortening, and skim milk that was chilled and mixed with flour before being fried. The details of today's recipe are top secret, though you can quickly tell by looking at the ingredient list that the current formula was concocted by a chemist, not some French chef. It's unlikely LeBoeuf would have even been able to pronounce calcium propionate or ethoxylated mono- and diglycerides, never mind knowing what to do with them.

But no matter where the recipe actually came from, we do know that in 1937, Rudolph decided to go into the donut business. According to company lore, the twenty-two-year-old and two buddies loaded up a shiny new Pontiac with donut-making equipment and, with $200 in savings in their collective pockets, hit the road. As they were hanging out one summer night in Peoria, Rudolph was fidgeting with a pack of Camels. Glancing at the package, he noticed that the cigarettes were manufactured in Winston-Salem, the home of R. J. Reynolds.

The cult of Krispy Kreme knows no class, race, or age barrier.

"Why not Winston-Salem?" asked Rudolph. "A town with a company producing a nationally advertised product has to be a good bet."

With the 750-mile trip behind them, the boys arrived in the North Carolina city with only twenty-five dollars left, just enough to rent an eighteen-foot-wide storefront on Main Street but not enough to buy any ingredients. They had to borrow the flour, potatoes, sugar, and milk from a local grocery store in order to make that first batch of Krispy Kremes on July 13, 1937. Using Rudolph's Pontiac for a delivery truck, they ferried the yeast-raised rings to grocery stores. They soon made enough money to repay the grocer who had fronted them the ingredients for the original batch. Within a decade, the fledgling entrepreneur had built the organization from a single outlet to a chain of stores in seven Southern states. By the time Rudolph died in 1973, the total number of stores had risen to sixty.

Krispy Kremes make a superior fashion accessory.

Krispy Kreme wasn't prepared for its founder's untimely end. Following his death, the company that some still compare to a Southern religion spent more than a decade wandering the wilderness. In 1976 it was bought by Beatrice Food only to be released from what many considered captivity in 1982 by a leveraged buyout led by its franchisees. There were some, the true believers, who believed Krispy Kreme should return to its roots, but for others, the bubbling economy of the 1980s was just too tempting. The management of the Southern donut chain set its eyes not merely on America but on the world. By the cusp of the millennium there were branches not only in New York but also Canada, England, the Philippines, Japan, and more than a dozen other spots around the globe. In the United States at least, this rapturous explosion of Krispy Kremes was just more than the market could sustain. When questions about its finances surfaced, the company's stock, which traded at almost fifty dollars in late 2003, dropped to one-tenth its value. Two hundred and forty stores were closed between 2004 and 2009. Even in New York, the shrines to fried dough had to shutter their gates. Where there were once nine Krispy Kremes in the Big Apple, there is now only a single sad branch stuck in the entrails of the Pennsylvania railway depot.

## GET THEM WHILE THEY'RE HAUTE

Though "the Appalachian love child of the soufflé and the croissant"—as *GQ* described the dough rings in 1996—wasn't able to satisfy capricious Manhattanites for long, the donut's sojourn in America's capital of hype left an impression. In New York, donuts, which had for so long been considered little more than working-class junk food, became the darlings of New York's manicured media elite. Soon after Krispy Kreme's arrival, fried dough started showing up on the menus of swanky restaurants.

# DONUTS IN THE PROMISED LAND

In 1975, Ted Ngoy, his wife Suganthini, and their three toddlers arrived at Southern California's Camp Pendleton. They were among the first Cambodian refugees that arrived in America following the murderous rise of Pol Pot in the aftermath of the Vietnam War. Penniless, the thirty-three-year-old Ngoy got a full-time position as a janitor at a nearby church. To make ends meet, he took on two more jobs: as the evening clerk at a local building-supply store and pumping gas at a neighborhood service station. As fate would have it, next door was a donut shop where Ngoy was introduced to the exotic treat. "I didn't know what it was, but I liked it," Ngoy later told a reporter for the *Los Angeles Times*. "I took some home and my kids liked it, too." He talked his way into a training program run by the Winchell's donut chain for aspiring managers. With his wife at his side, he worked seventeen-hour days managing a Winchell's in Newport Beach, eventually saving up enough to buy his own donut shop, Christy's. A dozen years later, that first Christy's had turned into fifty. Often employing other Cambodians who went on to open their own shops, Ngoy sowed the seeds of a phenomenon that lives on. According to some estimates, by the early years of the twenty-first century, Cambodians owned as many as 80 percent of California's independent donut shops.

This sort of ethnic dominance of donut shops isn't limited to Cambodians or to the Golden State. My neighborhood Dunkin' Donuts is run by South Asians, as is every second Dunkin' Donuts on the East Coast. But that's nothing compared to Chicago, where between them, Pakistanis and Indians own 95 percent of the pink-and-orange donut franchises. It's not that immigrants have gone into the donut business because they're more enamored of the American sinker than the fry cakes of their homelands, rather it's because the business has been relatively easy to get into. The ingredient costs are low, and you could count on family for free labor. Stinking of stale grease was just part of the dues that had to be paid for a shot at the American dream.

And what of Ted Ngoy? Sadly his success story did not have a happy ending. With the money from his donut business in his pocket he discovered Las Vegas and gradually gambled away every penny he made and then some, eventually borrowing and embezzling funds to feed his addiction. He lost his business, home, and family. By 2005, he was broke, homeless, and living off the kindness of his few remaining friends.

The upwardly mobile sinker didn't entirely appear out of a vacuum. There were glimmerings of a donut renaissance as early as 1991, when *Gourmet* magazine placed an old-fashioned basket of donuts on its cover. Nonetheless, the first yuppie donut can probably be traced to Thomas Keller, who started putting them on the menu at his pricey Napa Valley restaurant in 1994. Keller had just opened up the French Laundry early that summer, and the normally super-meticulous chef was having a little fun. Placing his well-practiced tongue firmly in cheek, he put "Coffee and Doughnuts" on the dessert menu. The dish consisted of a cappuccino semifreddo with "the best cinnamon-sugar doughnuts ever made," as the reviewer for the *San Francisco Chronicle* described them.

The smell of frying donuts must have been wafting through the zeitgeist that year, because even as Keller was putting the final touches on his award-winning restaurant in California, Mark Isreal was testing out recipes he would soon sell at his Lower East Side shop in New York. The thirty-one-year-old donut pioneer opened up a little storefront—rather ambitiously called the Doughnut Plant—in September 1994. The original operation was tiny. Initially, Isreal made only twelve dozen donuts a day, which he delivered on his bicycle to only three downtown retailers. In more ways than one, it was a labor of love, an homage to his grandfather who had once owned a bakery in Greensboro, North Carolina. If you put aside the wacky flavors, Isreal's donuts are in the Krispy Kreme mold; biting into them is like sinking your teeth into a warm, sugary cloud. Though if these are angels, they're of the fallen variety. What made Isreal's pastries special was that he applied an artisanal, locally sourced model to his dough rings. He didn't just deliver his creations on two wheels, he also rode up to the Union Square farmer's market where he'd buy fresh blackberries, peaches, and other ingredients for many of his creations. The recipe for the dough may have been Grandpa's, but the glazes were decidedly not. One of his early flavors, the Mary—named after his mother—was appliquéd with edible flowers and glazed with floral essence. For Valentine's Day, he made a heart-shaped donut with a passion-fruit glaze.

Coming in the wake of these two pioneers and the subsequent Manhattan Krispy Kreme apotheosis, the editors of *Food &Wine* magazine declared donuts the new "haute junk food" at the end of 1996. Soon enough, you could order *bomboloncini* (miniature cream-filled yeast-risen dough balls) at New York's trendy Italian-themed Osteria del Circo, or "drunken" donuts, which came with spiked jam, at the newly opened Maloney & Porcelli. Other haute treats followed, most notably on the menus of Danny Meyer's influential Union Square Café and its offspring. At Craft, the former Union Square Café chef Tom Colicchio began dishing up toylike stacks of donuts and holes with gooey caramel and chocolate sauce on the side. At Hearth, another restaurant tracing its genealogy to Danny Meyer, apple cider donuts were served with a slick of apple cider glaze and a dollop of whipped cream.

Where yuppies had gone before, the hipsters now followed. In Seattle, Top Pot fired up its fryers in 2002, with an upscale take on the Dunkin' Donuts model. Their densely cakey sinkers and barely chewy yeast-raised dough rings taste as if someone in the kitchen cares, but they certainly wouldn't challenge anyone's donut preconceptions. About the weirdest they go is a spiced chai model.

Other fried dough impresarios have been more off the wall. In the early days of the bacon-dessert fad, Voodoo Doughnuts made a name for itself with its bacon and maple bar, a slab of yeast-raised dough spread with maple frosting and topped with whole rashers of bacon. And that was one of its tamer flavors. When the Portland, Oregon, company first opened in 2003, they formulated both a Pepto-Bismol and a Robitussin donut—at least until the FDA put a stop to it. (You can't use medicine as an ingredient in food.) Nowadays the flavors are more sedate: the "blood" in the signature voodoo donut—a cartoonish chocolate-iced doughnut with arms, an iced toothy mouth, and a pretzel stick in its belly—is just plain old raspberry jelly; the triple chocolate penetration contains such ho-hum ingredients as

Compared to some of its other offerings, the Voodoo Doughnuts bacon maple bar is downright tame.

Cocoa Puffs. There is however a product that still makes Voodoo unique. Undoubtedly taking a cue from all the thousands who have served Krispy Kremes at their wedding, Voodoo offers legal weddings. If you pony up $325 for the deluxe wedding package, you get the ceremony, coffee and donuts for forty, and a donut centerpiece with the bride's and groom's names inscribed in the icing. And they'll even throw in free parking!

Over the last few years, hip donut shops have sprouted from sea to shining sea. In Philadelphia, Federal Donuts has been serving cake donuts scented with lavender and others filled with peanut butter and jelly; in Chicago, the Doughnut Vault boasts lemon poppy seed and pistachio; Denver's Glazed and Confuzed Doughnuts has made a valiant effort to push the envelope with a Red Bull–spiked sinker decorated with Pez candy and another spread with chipotle chocolate ganache and sprinkled with tortilla chips. In Austin, Gourdough's has busted the envelope wide open with the likes of the Boss Hog donut, mounded with pulled pork and potato salad, then drizzled with honey barbecue sauce.

As if too much wasn't enough, Epic Burgers and Waffles in Canada created the cronut burger.

In 2013, French pastry chef Dominique Ansel started serving his signature "cronuts" at his eponymous Soho bakery. The hype generated by these custard-filled donuts made with croissant dough led to anxious lines forming as early as dawn. I found it hard not to recall P.T. Barnum's famous line about his clientele. He was right, there really is one born every minute.

As in ancient Rome, our donut culture may be reaching a point of orgiastic decadence, which sooner or later will implode from sheer excess. Can a civilization survive the Luther Burger, a cheeseburger served on a split Krispy Kreme? Or a deluge of copycat cronuts? Perhaps not, but maybe once the Vandals (or the nutrition police) have razed and pillaged the nation's Dunkin' Donuts and Krispy Kremes, a time will come when we can all rediscover the joy of a simple cider donut. Or maybe not.

And anyway, by the time you read this, the hipster donut craze may be no more than an ironic footnote in the history of the donut's rise to world supremacy. Pulled pork, donuts, and Pepto-Bismol will be eaten separately, as three sequential courses, not consumed simultaneously in one donut recipe. More likely though, is that the artisanal sinker will join the millions that are being fried right now by Dunkin' Donuts, Krispy Kreme, Tim Hortons, and their like. And maybe that's just as well. As far as I'm concerned, when it comes to donuts, more is more.

# CONCLUSION

## *PONDERING THE CRUMBS*

After months of research and tasting the fried dough balls of four continents, I figured it was time to ask the big questions. So what is it that makes donuts so universally appealing? And what makes that sweet ring of fried dough so quintessentially American? I suspect we all instinctively know the answer to the first one, but since the whole point of this project was to have an excuse to eat donuts, I thought it best to ponder these profound questions with a donut and coffee in hand.

One of New York's favorite donut joints is Peter Pan Donuts and Bakery in the Greenpoint section of Brooklyn. The owners are of Greek extraction, though until recently the neighborhood was predominantly Polish. Nowadays, trendy professionals are moving in. In other words, it's as American as the donuts in the wire baskets that line the scuffed and faded wall.

I arrive at 9:15 on a foggy winter Monday morning. Outside, it's chilly and damp, but inside the crowd waiting to buy donuts is already spilling out the door. I squeeze between the African American cops chatting up the blonde Polish CVS manager, past the rumpled father with his little daughter and through the iPhone-engrossed hipsters. Thankfully, there are still a few spots at the worn Formica counters. Plopping onto a hard stool, I order a whole wheat and a red velvet to go with my coffee. Purely for purposes of research, mind you.

Finishing up the last few crumbs of the whole wheat donut, I begin to wonder what makes all these people crawl out of bed to wait patiently (or not so patiently) in line to get their donut fix? I've seen the scene before, in Seattle and Oakland, in Venice and Kolkata. Oh sure, the donuts have different names, and the recipe changes from place to place; but the

89

impatient crowd is much the same no matter the time zone. So what makes the donut such a worldwide object of desire?

I bite into my second donut—a red velvet—looking for clues. The appeal is direct and immediate. It's sweet, soft, and cakey; rich without being greasy; dissolving into delicate crumbs with every bite. It's also a little rough too, lumpy and eager to please, like a happy puppy. Let's face it, what's not to like? Certainly we are genetically programmed to crave sugar and fat, and with good evolutionary reason: both are densely packed with energy. And yes, donuts are indulgent, which makes them doubly desirable.

I realize that the people in line here, or for that matter at any neighborhood Dunkin' Donuts, are likely to have no knowledge of the donut's history. In a hurry to get to work in the morning, they could probably care less that the donut was once festival food, a treat eaten only on special occasions. I recall a conversation I had with Poppy Tooker, a lifelong New Orleanian and a Creole food maven. I was trying to make the connection between Mardi Gras and the local square donuts. She quickly disabused me of my delusion. While admitting that this may have been the case a couple of hundred years back, she assured me that it was not the case now. "They're a year-round New Orleans treat," she told me. "All of the places that serve beignets are open twenty-four hours a day, because beignets in New Orleans are an anytime food."

Which is basically true for fried dough in the rest of America too. Certainly most of us don't limit our donut consumption to a few days before Lent. (If America's waistline is any indication, all too many of us don't limit our donut consumption at all!) Our craving observes no season or special occasion. It is eaten by everyone irrespective of class, color, or creed. Yet even if in America, the pastry with a hole became decidedly ordinary, egalitarian, even democratic, it never lost its patina of indulgence.

It is this duality, I think, that explains the donut's appeal. Immigrants always saw the United States as a land of plenty, where food you might eat once or twice a year in the old country could be had every day. Back home, a German (or Mexican or Chinese) peasant might have seen meat once a week. Here, it was on the menu breakfast, lunch, and dinner. This was true of other foods as well, but none more so than the donut, the festival food par excellence, the holiday treat that we eat every day, the manna of the promised land. If there's a better nominee for an edible symbol of the American dream, I'd like to taste it.

Back in Brooklyn I'm riding a sugar high after my double dose of coffee and donuts. And I wonder if I'm not overanalyzing this. Maybe donuts are just donuts. With that in mind I ask for the bill—and a half dozen sour cream old-fashioneds for the road.

# DONUT RECIPES

~~~~~~~~~~~~~~~~~~~~~~~~~~~~~~~~~~~~~~~~~~~~~~~~~~~~~~~~~~~~~~~~~~~~~~

## FAT

When it comes down to it, as long as it's fat, you can fry in it. Around the world donuts have been fried in animal shortenings of every description. Clarified butter has long been considered superior for its flavor, but it was lard, aka hog fat, that used to be the most popular of all. Nineteenth-century sources often recommend goose fat, and cooks have even resorted to the fat rendered from sheep's tails and whales. On St. Pierre and Miquelon, the French islands off the coast of Newfoundland, seal oil is used to fry their Mardi Gras treats. And of course vegetable oil of every origin is ubiquitous.

In my experience, lard and other fats that stay solid at room temperature (such as vegetable shortening) make the donuts crisper and appear less greasy. The downside, especially with vegetable shortening, is that they give the pastry a slightly chalky aftertaste. Oil is much easier to deal with, but be careful: not all oils are created equal. Some, like soybean oil, leave a heavy, greasy aftertaste, while others, like corn, peanut, and olive oil, impart their own very specific flavor. Even so-called flavorless oils have some flavor. I find canola oil makes everything taste slightly fishy. My favorite oils to fry with are grapeseed, sunflower, and safflower oil. Make sure they are not "raw" or "virgin." These oils have a low smoke point and are dangerous to use in deep-frying. Oil can be reused up to a half dozen times if it's only used for frying donuts. Just make sure to cool and filter it between each use.

## FRYING TIPS

For frying donuts, a deep fryer with a built-in thermostat and basket that allows you to lift and drain the donuts without fuss makes the process of preparing donuts immeasurably easier. If this is not available, use a heavy pan—cast-iron is ideal—with at least five-inch sides and a deep-fry thermometer that allows you to monitor the frying temperature. When frying, don't crowd the pan. Keep in mind that the donuts will expand during frying, and you don't want them to touch. Always make sure that the temperature rises to the correct level specified in the recipe between batches. If the fat is too cool, your donuts will be greasy. Once they are fried, drain well on a cooling rack. With some recipes it's helpful to line the cooling rack with paper towels to absorb the excess grease.

## TOPPING YOUR DONUT

Once the donuts are cooked, you have several choices. You can toss them in granulated sugar while they're still warm, wait until they cool and dust them with confectioners' sugar, or you can glaze or ice them. The difference between the last two is really no more than the thickness of the topping. Glazes are relatively thin, and the donuts should be dipped in them while still warm. The result is a mostly transparent, well, glaze. Icings are a smidgeon thicker and should be applied once the donut is cool. You can turn one into the other by whisking in a little more confectioners' sugar to thicken it or adding a few drops of boiling water to thin it out. In either case, the glazes and icings themselves should be warm when you use them. The terrific thing about either is that you can play with both colors and flavors to your heart's content. Fruit juices and purees, liqueurs, and any number of extracts can be added to the icings and frostings. Fancy a little color? Add a drop or two of orange food coloring for Halloween or stripe the donuts with red, white, and blue for the Fourth of July. As far as toppings go, these work better with icings, but use them within a minute or two of icing, otherwise they won't adhere well.

# FASCHINGSKRAPFEN: CARNIVAL JELLY DONUTS

As nineteenth-century celebrity chef F. G. Zenker explained in his 1824 cookbook *Der Zuckerbäcker Für Frauen Mittlerer Stände* (*Confectionary for Middle Class Ladies*), lightness is everything. Viennese Carnival donuts must be so ethereal that they do not sink more than halfway into the hot lard; this is how they receive the characteristic pale ring around their middles. There used to be a time when you would find these only for Carnival (*Fasching*), but these days, every bakery and café has them year-round. The most traditional filling is apricot preserves, but there is no reason that you can't use raspberry, strawberry, or any other flavor you choose. Lemon curd, for example, is one of my favorites.

*Makes 20 jelly donuts*

½ ounce (2 envelopes) active dry yeast

2 cups plus 2 tablespoons lukewarm milk (about 105°F), divided

1¾ ounces (about 3 tablespoons plus 1 teaspoon) sugar, divided

2 pounds 3 ounces (about 8 cups) unbleached all-purpose flour
    (plus a handful more to roll out dough)

6 large egg yolks

3½ ounces (7 tablespoons) unsalted butter, melted and cooled

Large pinch of salt

½ cup apricot preserves

About 2 tablespoons melted butter to brush with

Oil or shortening for frying

Confectioners' sugar

1. In a small bowl, combine the yeast, ¼ cup warmed milk, and 1 teaspoon sugar. Stir to dissolve. Stir in 2 ounces (about ½ cup) flour. Cover this "sponge" with plastic wrap and let rise in a warm place until doubled in volume, about 20 minutes.

2. In a separate bowl, whisk the yolks until frothy. Gradually, whisk in the melted butter.

3. Transfer the risen sponge to the bowl of a stand mixer fitted with a paddle attachment. On medium-low speed, beat in the egg mixture, the remainder of the milk and sugar, then about half the flour. Switch to a dough hook attachment, gradually add the remaining flour and, finally, the salt. Beat on medium-low speed until the dough is smooth, shiny, and elastic, about 5 minutes.

4. Remove the dough from the bowl and set on a floured surface. Knead very briefly to turn it into a ball. Set in a buttered bowl, cover with plastic wrap, and let rise in a warm place until doubled in volume, about 45 minutes.

5. Using a rolling pin, roll the dough on a floured surface until it is a little less than ¼-inch thick. Then, using a 2¼-inch-diameter cookie or biscuit cutter, cut out as many circles as you can. Gather up the scraps and roll out the dough one more time, cutting out more circles. This is easier if you let gathered-up scraps rest for 5 minutes before rerolling.

6. Brush the edge of each round with a little water. Spread every other circle with about a scant teaspoon of preserves to within ½ inch of the edge. Top each with a plain circle, making sure the moistened edges touch. Press the edges lightly to help the dough adhere. Using a 2-inch cookie or biscuit cutter dipped in flour, cut out each donut once more, discarding the trimmings.

7. Brush these lightly with melted butter on each side. Set on a baking sheet lined with parchment paper and cover loosely with plastic wrap. Let rise until they are about 50 percent larger—any more than that, and they will expand too much during frying.

8. Heat at least 2 inches of oil or shortening in a deep pan to 350°F. If you're not using a deep fryer with a built-in thermostat, check the temperature using a candy or deep-fry thermometer. (See Frying Tips, p. 92.) Slide in the donuts, one by one, making sure not to crowd the pan. Fry until the underside is light brown, about 1½ minutes. Turn the donut and cook until the other side is brown, about 1 minute. There should be a pale "collar" around the middle of the donut where it floated above the fat.

9. With a slotted spoon, lift out the cooked donuts and drain on a cooling rack set above a baking pan or on paper towels. Dust with confectioners' sugar just before serving.

# OLIEBOLLEN: DUTCH DONUTS

Whereas most Europeans eat their donuts during Carnival, the Dutch indulge in their treats a few weeks earlier, at New Year's. According to legend, this is an old Germanic tradition that dates back to the pagan worship of the goddess Perchta, whose feast coincided with Epiphany. More likely it was just a way to indulge in the winter holiday period following Christmas. While it seems likely that the Dutch shared the fried dough tradition of their German neighbors as far back as the Middle Ages, the current recipe for *oliebollen* (literally "oil balls"), scented with Eastern spices and chock-full of raisins or currants, may have been picked up by Dutch traders in the Renaissance. Some Dutch food historians even think the fritters were introduced by the Spanish (who controlled the Netherlands for a time) or Spanish Jews fleeing the Inquisition. The fritters are also very much like what you find in Venice, though this may simply be a matter of great minds thinking alike. The earliest recipe for what were then known as *olie-koeken* (oil-cakes) dates back to a cookbook from 1668, and we know that at least one Dutch immigrant brought that recipe collection to the New World. In Holland today, there are countless variations on the recipe. This particular version uses both yeast and beer to give the balls lift. Use a Belgian-style Trappist beer like Chimay Dubbel to make the dough balls extra tasty. If one of those is unavailable, find yourself a malt-rich brown ale; Guinness works too.

*Makes about 36 donuts*

4 ounces (about ¾ cup) raisins

⅓ cup orange juice

3 tablespoons dark rum

¼ cup lukewarm milk (about 105°F)

¼ ounce (1 packet) active dry yeast

9 ounces (about 2 cups), unbleached all-purpose flour, divided

⅔ cup dark beer at room temperature

1 egg

¼ teaspoon salt

1 ounce (2 tablespoons) sugar

4 ounces peeled and cored apple, cut into ¼-inch dice (about 1 cup)

1 teaspoon ground cinnamon

Oil or shortening for frying

Confectioners' sugar for dusting

1. Combine the raisins, orange juice, and rum in a small bowl. Cover and let stand overnight at room temperature. Drain.

2. In the bowl of a stand mixer, stir together the warm milk and yeast. Let stand 5 minutes. Stir in 2 ounces (about ½ cup) flour. Cover with plastic wrap and let stand until bubbly and doubled in volume, about ½ hour. Stir in the beer and egg. In a separate bowl, mix together the remaining flour, salt, and granulated sugar.

3. Using a paddle attachment, on low speed, beat the flour mixture into the beer mixture. Beat for 5 minutes on medium speed to make the batter very smooth. It should be somewhat thicker than pancake batter. Stir in the drained raisins, apples, and cinnamon.

4. Cover the bowl with plastic wrap and put in a warm place to rise. Let stand until the batter has doubled in volume, anywhere from an hour to an hour and a half.

5. Using a deep fryer or a heavy pan, heat at least 3 inches of the oil or shortening to 350°F. If you're not using a deep fryer with a built-in thermostat, check the temperature using a candy or deep-fry thermometer. (See Frying Tips, p.92.)

6. Lightly oil two tablespoons. Scoop about 2 tablespoons batter in one spoon, and slide the dough off and into the hot fat with the second. A small oiled ice cream scoop works well too. Fry about a half dozen at a time, turning occasionally until cooked through, about 4 minutes total. Drain and allow to cool enough so you can pick them up. Sprinkle generously with confectioners' sugar. The *oliebollen* are best served warm. Leftovers can be frozen and reheated in a 350°F oven.

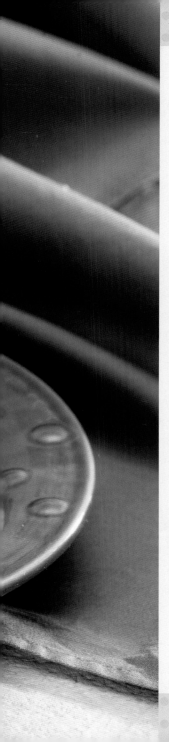

# ZALABIA:
# SYRIAN HANUKKAH FRITTERS

The idea of dipping little donuts into honey goes back at least a couple of thousand years. When the Persians and Arabs adapted the recipe in the early Middle Ages, they substituted sugar syrup, which is still mostly what is used throughout the Middle East and North Africa. Today, each of the Abrahamic religions fries these up for one celebration or another. In Islam, they are common for ending the fast during Ramadan, but you'll also find them eaten during Mawlid, the holiday honoring the birth of the prophet Muhammad. In Lebanon, Christians make them for Epiphany. Appropriately enough, Syrian Jews adopted the fried dough balls for Hanukkah, the holiday that celebrates the miracle of sacred oil. My suggestion, if you wish to promote world peace, is to make these for all of the above.

*Makes 4 dozen donuts*

SYRUP:

1 pound (about 2 cups) sugar

⅔ cup water

1½ teaspoons lemon juice

1½ teaspoons rosewater or orange blossom water

FRITTER DOUGH:

1 cup lukewarm water (about 105°F)

¼ ounce (1 packet) active dry yeast

10 ounces (about 2¼ cups) bleached all-purpose flour

1 ounce (about 2 tablespoons) sugar

¼ teaspoon salt

Oil for frying

1. Make the syrup: Combine 1 pound sugar and ⅔ cup water in a small saucepan. Bring to a boil and stir until the sugar is completely dissolved. Simmer until the syrup is the consistency of hot honey, about 5 minutes. Remove from heat and cool to room temperature. Stir in the lemon juice and rosewater or orange blossom water.

2. Make the batter: In the bowl of a stand mixer fitted with a paddle attachment, combine the lukewarm water and yeast. In a separate bowl, whisk together the flour, 1 ounce sugar, and salt. Gradually beat in the flour mixture. Mix until smooth and a little elastic. Cover with plastic wrap, and let rise in a warm place until double original volume, about 45 minutes. Uncover, and beat once more. Cover, and let rise again, about 30 minutes.

3. Using a deep fryer or a heavy pan, heat at least 3 inches of the oil to 360°F. If you're not using a deep fryer with a built-in thermostat, check the temperature using a candy or deep-fry thermometer. (See Frying Tips, p.92.)

4. Dip two teaspoons in a small bowl of oil to coat. Working in batches, spoon about a teaspoon of batter at a time into the hot oil. Fry, turning occasionally, until puffed, crisp, and golden, about 5 minutes. The light batter produces irregular, rather than round, fritters.

5. Using a slotted spoon, remove fritters and transfer to a paper towel–lined baking sheet to drain. Warm the syrup to lukewarm. Dip fritters in the warm syrup for about 30 seconds to coat and soak up some syrup. Don't leave them in too long, though, or they will get soggy. Serve warm or at room temperature.

# WHOLE WHEAT APPLE CIDER DONUTS

Many commercially produced donuts are made with a batter that is too wet to roll. This results in lighter pastry but requires a donut extruder. One technique that I learned from the donut bakers at the Cartems Donuterie in Vancouver is that you can get away with using a wetter dough if you use a piping bag to "extrude" the donuts. This also gives you the option of making the donuts any diameter you like. You will need a heavy pastry bag fitted with a ½-inch plain tip, and, once formed, the donuts are much easier to handle if you chill them for an hour or two in the refrigerator.

*Makes about 16 donuts*

DONUT DOUGH:

1 ½ cups apple cider

½ cup milk

1 teaspoon pure vanilla extract

8 ounces (about 1 ¾ cups) bleached all-purpose flour

4 ½ ounces (about 1 cup) whole wheat flour

1 tablespoon baking powder

½ teaspoon salt

½ teaspoon cinnamon

Large pinch grated nutmeg

Large pinch grated cloves

5 ounces (about ⅔ cup) raw (turbinado) sugar or substitute light brown sugar

1½ ounces (3 tablespoons) unsalted butter, softened

1 large egg, at room temperature

1 egg yolk, at room temperature

Oil or shortening for frying


CINNAMON SUGAR:

4 ounces (about ½ cup) sugar

1 tablespoon ground cinnamon


1. In a small saucepan, boil the cider until it is reduced to ¼ cup. Cool.

2. Line two sheet pans with parchment paper and spray lightly with vegetable spray. In a measuring cup, stir together the milk, reduced cider, and vanilla. It will look curdled. In a medium bowl, whisk together the flours, baking powder, salt, and spices.

3. In a stand mixer fitted with a paddle attachment, beat the sugar and butter until well incorporated, about 1 minute. Add the egg and egg yolk and beat until fluffy, smooth, and pale, 2 to 3 minutes.

4. Alternating, add the milk and flour mixtures into the egg mixture in 2 or 3 additions, beating on low speed until just barely combined between each addition. Stir until the mixture just comes together to make a soft, sticky dough. Do not overbeat or it will get tough.

5. Working with about half the dough at a time, fill a piping bag fitted with a ½-inch plain tip. Pipe circles of dough about 3 inches in diameter on the parchment. Repeat with the remaining dough. If you wish, you can smooth the seam with a damp finger. Cover with plastic wrap and refrigerate at least 1 hour and up to 6 hours. Remove plastic wrap, lightly dust the donuts with flour, place another pan over each pan, and invert. Carefully peel off the parchment paper.

6. Using a deep fryer or a heavy pan, heat at least 3 inches of the oil or shortening to 360°F. If you're not using a deep fryer with a built-in thermostat, check the temperature using a candy or deep-fry thermometer. (See Frying Tips, p. 92.) Drop several donuts at a time into the heated fat, making sure there is enough room for all of them to float to the surface. Cook 30 to 45 seconds per side, using a slotted spoon or tongs to turn each donut. When golden brown, transfer the donuts to a cooling rack covered with paper towels. Cool to just above room temperature.

7. Whisk together the granulated sugar and 1 tablespoon cinnamon in a wide bowl. Toss the barely warm donuts in the cinnamon sugar mixture, and serve warm.

# FRITTELLE DI CARNEVALE: VENETIAN CARNIVAL FRITTERS

The earliest recipe for these appears as early as 1570 in a cookbook penned by the papal cook, Bartolomeo Scappi. He calls them *frittelle alla veneziana*. They were unfilled, but given the lifestyle of the pontiffs in those days, I'm sure they wouldn't have objected to a little boozy, creamy filling. After all, *vinsanto* (a sweet wine made from partially desiccated grapes) means "holy wine" in Italian. If you can't get ahold of *vinsanto*, use sweet Marsala. Chances are His Holiness won't notice the difference.

*Makes about 2 dozen* frittelle

ZABAGLIONE FILLING:

⅓ cup *vinsanto* or sweet Marsala

2 tablespoons dark rum

1 teaspoon unflavored gelatin

3 egg yolks

2½ ounces (about ⅓ cup) sugar

1½ cups heavy or whipping cream

FRITTELLE DOUGH:

1 cup water

2 ounces (4 tablespoons) unsalted butter, cut into pieces

¼ teaspoon salt

4½ ounces (about 1 cup) bleached all-purpose flour

4 large eggs

Oil or shortening for frying

Confectioners' sugar for dusting

1. Make the zabaglione filling: Combine the *vinsanto*, rum, and gelatin in metal bowl. Let stand 10 minutes and then set over very low heat or a small saucepan of simmering water and stir until the gelatin is fully dissolved.

2. In a separate metal bowl, beat the egg yolks and sugar until thoroughly combined. Gradually stir in the warm rum mixture. Place over very low heat or over a double boiler and whisk gently but continually until light and fluffy, about 5 minutes. Do not cook too long or the eggs will coagulate! Keep whisking for about a minute once you've removed it from the heat, and then set aside and let cool to room temperature. With an electric mixer, whip the cream until it holds soft peaks. Fold into the egg mixture in two additions with a rubber spatula. Chill.

3. Make the *frittelle* dough: Combine 1 cup water, the butter, and salt in a heavy saucepan. Bring to a boil. When the butter melts, add the flour all at once. Stir with a wooden spoon over low heat about 5 minutes. The dough should be soft and should not stick to your fingers.

4. Transfer the dough to a bowl. Let the dough cool 5 minutes. Add the eggs one at a time, beating until each egg is fully incorporated before adding the next. This is easiest done in a food processor or stand mixer.

5. Using a deep fryer or a heavy pan, heat at least 3 inches of the oil or shortening to 370°F. If you're not using a deep fryer with a built-in thermostat, check the temperature using a candy or deep-fry thermometer. (See Frying Tips, p. 92.)

6. Using 2 lightly oiled tablespoons or a mini ice cream scoop, scoop and form small balls of dough about 1 inch in diameter. Drop these into the fat and fry 10 to 12 minutes, until golden, puffed, and cooked through. Turn the balls occasionally to ensure even frying. Drain on paper towels. Let cool to room temperature.

7. Transfer the zabaglione filling to a piping bag fitted with a ¼-inch plain tip. Fill the *frittelle* by punching a small hole in one side of each with a small knife and piping in the filling. Fill each fritter until it feels heavy and the filling begins to come out of the hole. To serve, sprinkle with confectioners' sugar.

# CHOCOLATE-GLAZED BISMARCKS WITH MARSHMALLOW CREAM

A Bismarck is nothing more than a jelly donut. Presumably it got its moniker in the late nineteenth century, when the German chancellor Otto von Bismarck was a household name and jelly donuts were still associated with German immigrants. I suppose you could also call these Boston creams, even if the filling isn't the traditional custard, which of course you could use instead of the marshmallow filling. For filling them, you ideally want a piping bag fitted with a Bismarck tip (it looks like a miniature funnel) with a ¼-inch opening, though a ¼-inch plain tip will do in a pinch.

*Makes a baker's dozen donuts*

DONUT DOUGH:

1 cup lukewarm milk (about 105°F)

¼ ounce (1 packet) active dry yeast

2 ounces (¼ cup) sugar, divided

9 ounces (about 2 cups) unbleached all-purpose flour

2 ounces (about ⅓ cup) potato flour

1 teaspoon salt

1 ounce (2 tablespoons) unsalted butter, at room temperature

1 large egg

1 teaspoon pure vanilla extract

Large pinch nutmeg

Oil or shortening for frying

MARSHMALLOW CREAM:

¼ cup water

1 teaspoon unflavored gelatin

3 large egg whites

12 ounces (about 1½ cups) sugar

Pinch of salt

½ teaspoon pure vanilla extract

Fudgy Chocolate Icing (see following recipe)

1. Make the donuts: Whisk the milk, yeast, and 1 teaspoon sugar together in the bowl of a stand mixer and set aside for 5 minutes.

2. In a large bowl, whisk together the remaining sugar, all-purpose flour, potato flour, and salt. Set aside.

3. Add the butter, egg, and vanilla to the foaming yeast mixture. Mix with the paddle attachment on low speed to break up the butter, about 1 minute. Add about a third of the dry ingredients and mix until blended on low speed. Repeat with the second third of the dry ingredients.

4. Switch to the dough hook, and then add the remaining dry ingredients and nutmeg, mixing on low speed until no flour remains each time. Add additional flour until the dough is dry enough to mostly clean the bottom of the bowl. Increase speed to medium and knead for 2 more minutes. (It should be smooth like bread dough but still a little tacky.)

5. Transfer the dough to a baking sheet sprinkled with about 1 tablespoon flour. Shape the dough into a flat disk 6 inches in diameter, dust lightly with flour, cover with plastic wrap, and set aside. Let the dough rise at room temperature until double in volume, about 45 minutes.

6. Transfer the disk of dough to a lightly floured board without kneading it or reshaping it. Roll to ½-inch thickness. Let it rest 5 minutes before cutting to prevent it from shrinking up. Using a 2½-inch round cutter, cut the dough into rounds, flouring the cutter before each cut. Gather up the remaining dough into a ball. Let rest 5 minutes and then roll out again for additional donuts. Transfer the donuts to two baking sheets, each sprinkled with about 2 tablespoons flour, arranging them at least 2 inches apart. Cover loosely with plastic wrap and let rise at room temperature until doubled in size, 45 minutes to 1 hour.

7. Using a deep fryer or a heavy pan, heat at least 2 inches of the oil or shortening to 375°F. If you're not using a deep fryer with a built-in thermostat, check the temperature using a candy or deep-fry thermometer. (See Frying Tips, p.92.)

8. When the donuts have doubled in size, carefully place a few in the oil, taking care not to overcrowd them. Fry until light golden brown on the bottom, about 1 minute. (Keep in mind that the donuts will look darker once they're done than they do in the oil.) Carefully turn the donuts and fry until golden on the second side, about 45 seconds. Cool, rounded-side up, on a rack lined with paper towels, until they are a little warmer than room temperature.

9. Once the donuts are fried, make the marshmallow filling: Pour the water into a heatproof bowl and sprinkle with the gelatin. Let stand 5 minutes. Add the egg whites, sugar, and salt. Whisk until smooth. Set the bowl over (not in) a saucepan of simmering water. Cook over medium heat, stirring constantly, until sugar has dissolved (or mixture registers 160°F on an instant-read thermometer), about 2 to 3 minutes. Transfer gelatin mixture to the bowl of a stand mixer. Add vanilla. Using the whisk attachment for your mixer, beat on high until the mixture is thick and glossy and has cooled to room temperature, about 5 minutes. The filling should have the consistency of soft whipped cream. Use immediately, otherwise the filling will begin to set.

10. Fill the donuts while they're still a little warm: Using a sharp, narrow knife, make a horizontal incision in the side of each donut, and pivot back and forth a little to make a pocket in the center of the donut without increasing the size of the opening. Spoon about 1½ cups of the filling into a piping bag fitted with a Bismarck tip. Insert the tube of the tip fully into the donut and squeeze about 2 tablespoons of the filling into each donut. Wipe off the excess with a damp paper towel.

11. Once donuts are filled, make the Fudgy Chocolate Icing. When ready, dip the top of each donut in the very warm icing. Set the donuts icing-side up on a wire rack so icing can harden, about 30 minutes.

# FUDGY CHOCOLATE ICING

*makes about 1 cup, enough to ice a baker's dozen donuts*

¼ cup water

3 ounces (about 6 tablespoons) sugar

3 ounces bittersweet chocolate, chopped

Combine the water and sugar in a small nonreactive saucepan. Bring to a boil and cook at a steady simmer for 2 minutes (no more) until the sugar is thoroughly dissolved. Using a whisk, gently stir in the chocolate. You want to avoid air bubbles. The glaze should coat the back of a spoon with about an ⅛ inch of the glaze. Cool about 1 minute. Use while still very warm.

# PUMPKIN DONUTS WITH MAPLE SYRUP GLAZE

In the early twentieth century, Halloween meant apples and donuts at least as much as candy. One popular game was to have the little goblins bob for donuts—that is, hang the sinkers on a string and try to eat one hands-free. And what could be better than a little pumpkin in the dough? OK, I'm cheating here and not really using pumpkin. But it's all for a good cause. I've found that if I use the widely available kabocha squash, the donuts taste more "pumpkiny" than if I use the real thing. Just think of it as a little trick that improves the treat. You won't need a whole squash (they usually come in at about 2½ pounds), so cut it in half, use one half for the recipe and serve the rest roasted with dinner. As far as the glaze goes, you want to find the darkest maple syrup possible; grade B is ideal.

*Makes 1½ dozen donuts*

About 1¼ pounds of kabocha squash (half of a 2½-pound squash)

12 ounces (about 3 cups) cake flour

1 tablespoon baking powder

½ teaspoon salt

¼ teaspoon grated nutmeg

1 teaspoon ground cinnamon

Large pinch ground cloves

½ teaspoon ground ginger

¼ teaspoon turmeric

½ cup milk

½ teaspoon pure vanilla extract

3 ounces (about ½ cup) light brown sugar

1 ounce (2 tablespoons) unsalted butter, softened

2 large egg yolks

Oil or shortening for frying

Maple Syrup Glaze (see following recipe)

1. Preheat oven to 350°F. Scoop out the seeds from the squash, wrap tightly in foil. Set on a baking sheet and bake until very tender, about 1 hour. Cool, scoop out the flesh, and puree in a food processor. Measure 8½ ounces (about 1 cup) of the puree and reserve.

2. Sift the flour, baking powder, salt, and spices together in a medium bowl and set aside. In a small bowl, whisk together the squash, milk, and vanilla.

3. In a stand mixer fitted with the paddle attachment, mix the sugar and butter on medium speed, until homogenous, about 1 minute. Add the egg yolks. Mix on medium speed, periodically scraping the sides of the bowl with a rubber spatula, until the mixture is very smooth and a couple of shades lighter, about 5 minutes.

4. Add the flour mixture to the beaten egg mixture in three additions, each time alternating with the squash. After each addition, mix on low speed until just combined, and scrape the sides of the bowl. The dough will be very sticky, like thick cake dough.

5. Line two sheet pans with parchment paper. Spray with nonstick vegetable spray. Working with about half the dough at a time, fill a piping bag fitted with a ½-inch plain tip. Pipe circles about 4 inches in diameter on the parchment. Repeat with

the remaining dough. Using a dampened finger, smooth the seams. Cover loosely with plastic wrap and refrigerate for at least 1 hour and up to 6 hours.

6. Using a deep fryer or a heavy pan, heat at least 3 inches of oil or shortening to 375°F. If you're not using a deep fryer with a built-in thermostat, check the temperature using a candy or deep-fry thermometer. (See Frying Tips, p. 92.)

7. Remove the plastic wrap. Sprinkle the donuts very lightly with flour. Place another pan over each donut pan and invert. Carefully peel the parchment off the donuts.

8. Add the donuts to the hot fat, a few at a time, taking care not to crowd them. Once the donuts float, fry until deep golden brown on both sides, about 45 seconds per side. Drain on a cooling rack. While the donuts are still very warm, dip the more attractive side of each in the glaze. Let drip briefly, then set back on the cooling rack, glazed-side up, to dry at least 15 minutes before serving. If the glaze seems too thick, stir in a few drops of boiling water to make for easier dipping.

## MAPLE SYRUP GLAZE

*Makes about ¾ cup glaze, enough to glaze the top of about 1½ dozen donuts.*

½ cup maple syrup (preferably grade B)

4 ounces (about 1 cup) confectioners' sugar

Briefly heat the maple syrup in a small pan or in a microwave-safe dish in the microwave. It should just begin to bubble. Transfer the maple syrup to a medium bowl and whisk in the confectioners' sugar until smooth. Use while still warm. If the glaze seems too thick, stir in a few drops of boiling water.

# MEXICAN CHOCOLATE CHURROS

Churros have been around for hundreds of years and maybe even thousands if you include the churro-like recipe in an ancient Roman cookbook attributed to Apicius. The name, however, comes into print only in the late 1800s, and the use may be Latin American in origin. Originally, *churro* referred to a kind of coarse wool, so perhaps someone thought the rough strands of fried dough looked a little like it. If you're looking for a little more authenticity, use Ceylon cinnamon, or what Latin American shops call *canela*, rather than the cinnamon sold in mainstream supermarkets. They aren't entirely the same spice. These churros are tasty on their own, but if you wish to gild the lily, serve these with a puddle of warm dulce de leche (see recipe p. 131).

*Makes about 3 dozen churros*

## CINNAMON SUGAR:

8 ounces (about 1 cup) sugar

2 teaspoons ground cinnamon

## CHURRO DOUGH:

1¼ cups water

1 ounce (2 tablespoons) unsalted butter

½ teaspoon salt

5 ounces (about 1 cup plus 2 tablespoons) bleached all-purpose flour, sifted

3 tablespoons Dutch process cocoa

½ teaspoon pure vanilla extract

½ teaspoon ground cinnamon

2 large eggs

Oil or shortening for frying

1. Make the cinnamon sugar: In a small bowl, whisk together the sugar and 2 teaspoons cinnamon.

2. Make the churro dough: In a medium saucepan over moderate heat, combine the water, butter, and salt. Bring to a simmer, stirring to melt the butter. Remove the pot from the heat and add the flour, stirring vigorously to fully incorporate it into the liquid. Return the pot to moderate heat and cook the mixture, stirring constantly, until the dough is smooth and no longer sticks to the sides of the pan, about 1 minute. Remove from the heat and let cool 5 minutes.

3. Transfer dough to a food processor. Add the cocoa, vanilla, and ½ teaspoon cinnamon and pulse to incorporate. Add 1 egg and process until completely smooth. Add the other egg and do the same. Scrape the sides and process once more to make sure the mixture is homogenous. Scrape into a bowl, cover with plastic wrap, and cool to room temperature. Chill in the refrigerator. The recipe can be made up to 24 hours ahead to this point.

4. Spoon the dough into a pastry bag fitted with a ½-inch closed star tip.

5. Fry the churros: Line a large baking sheet with several layers of paper towels and place the cinnamon sugar in a wide shallow bowl.

6. Using a deep fryer or a heavy pan, heat at least 3 inches of oil or shortening to 375°F. If you're not using a deep fryer with a built-in thermostat, check the temperature using a candy or deep-fry thermometer. (See Frying Tips, p.92.)

7. Working in batches (about 6 churros per batch), hold the pastry bag just above the surface of the hot fat and carefully pipe 4- to 5-inch lengths of dough directly into the fat, using a small knife to cut the batter at the end of the star tip if necessary. Fry the churros, turning occasionally, until crispy and cooked in the center, about 3 minutes. When done, transfer to the paper towel–lined baking sheet. Cool to room temperature. Toss the churros gently in the cinnamon sugar.

# DULCE DE LECHE RAISED DONUTS WITH SALTY CARAMEL GLAZE

I happen to adore caramel in all of its many incarnations—almost as much as donuts. Here, I've combined two very different forms of caramelized sugar for a sort of one-two punch that is further emphasized by a teeny sprinkle of salt at the very end. You ideally want a flaked salt like fleur de sel, which will add a complex salinity to the sweet and bitter caramel.

*Makes about 1½ dozen donuts*

¾ ounce (3 packets) active dry yeast

¾ cup lukewarm water (about 105°F)

14 ounces (about 3 cups) bread flour, divided, plus more for rolling and cutting

1 teaspoon ground cinnamon

1 teaspoon salt

⅔ cup dulce de leche (see note on p. 131)

2 ounces (4 tablespoons) unsalted butter at room temperature

3 large egg yolks

1 teaspoon pure vanilla extract

Oil or shortening for frying

Caramel Glaze (see following recipe)

Fleur de sel or similar flaked salt

1. Stir the yeast and water together in the work bowl of a stand mixer and set aside for 5 minutes. Stir in 3 ounces (about ¾ cup) of the flour and let stand until the mixture is bubbly and has doubled in volume, about 15 minutes.

2. In a large bowl, whisk together the remaining flour, cinnamon, and salt. Set aside.

3. Add the dulce de leche, butter, egg yolks, and vanilla to the foaming yeast mixture. Mix with the paddle attachment on low speed to break up the butter, about 1 minute. Add about a third of the dry ingredients and mix on low speed until blended. Repeat with the second third of the dry ingredients.

4. Switch to the dough hook and add the remaining dry ingredients, mixing on low speed until no spots of flour remain each time, adding remaining flour until the dough is dry enough not to stick to the bottom of the bowl. Increase speed to medium and knead for 2 more minutes. (It should be smooth like bread dough, but still a little tacky.)

5. Transfer the dough to a baking sheet sprinkled with about 1 tablespoon flour, shape into a flat disk 6 inches in diameter, dust lightly with flour, cover with a plastic wrap, and let the dough rise at room temperature until double in volume, about 1 hour.

6. Transfer the risen dough to a lightly floured work surface and roll with a lightly floured rolling pin into a roughly 12-inch circle about ½-inch thick. Using a 3-inch donut cutter, cut the dough into about 12 rings, making sure to dust the cutter with flour before each cut. Gather up the leftover dough into a ball. Let rest 5 minutes, and then roll again for additional donuts. Transfer the donuts to two baking sheets each sprinkled with about 2 tablespoons flour, arranging them at least 2 inches apart. Spray plastic wrap lightly with vegetable spray and cover the donuts, sprayed-side down, with the plastic. Let them rise until doubled in size, about 1 hour. Carefully remove the plastic wrap.

7. Using a deep fryer or a heavy pan, heat at least 2 inches of the oil or shortening to 370°F. If you're not using a deep fryer with a built-in thermostat, check the temperature using a candy or deep-fry thermometer. (See Frying Tips, p. 92.)

8. When the donuts have doubled in size, carefully place a few in the fat, taking care not to overcrowd them, and fry until light golden brown on the bottom, about 30 seconds. (Keep in mind that the donuts will look darker once they're done than they do in the fat.) Carefully turn the donuts and fry until golden on the second side, 20 to 30 seconds. Cool, rounded-side up on a rack placed over a layer of paper towels.

9. While the donuts are still warm, dip the rounded side of each into the warm Salty Caramel Glaze. Sprinkle very lightly with the fleur de sel. Let dry on racks, glazed-side up, for 10 to 15 minutes before serving.

Note: While you can certainly buy dulce de leche, making it is easy, if time consuming. The simplest way to do it is to buy a can of (sweetened) condensed milk, scrape the contents into an 8-by-8-inch Pyrex pan, and cover tightly with foil. Set this pan in a roasting pan, and pour boiling water into the larger pan so that it reaches about halfway up the sides of the Pyrex pan. Set in a 350°F oven and bake about 2 hours, adding more hot water if it gets too low. The longer you cook it, the more caramelized it will become. When it reaches the desired color, remove from the oven and whisk until smooth. Store in a glass jar. It will last months in the refrigerator. If it gets too thick, whisk in a few drops of hot water.

## SALTY CARAMEL GLAZE

*Makes ¾ cup glaze, enough to glaze about 1½ dozen donuts*

¼ cup sugar
5 tablespoons water, divided
6 ounces (about 1½ cups) confectioners' sugar
½ teaspoon pure vanilla extract
¼ teaspoon salt

1. Combine the granulated sugar with 2 tablespoons water in a small saucepan. Bring to a boil and cook until all the water has evaporated and the sugar begins to caramelize. Do not stir. Once the caramel is dark amber, remove from heat and let stand 1 minute. Add remaining 3 tablespoons water, place back on the heat, and simmer, stirring gently, until the caramel is dissolved. Transfer to a bowl.

2. While still hot, whisk in the confectioners' sugar and then the vanilla. If the glaze is too thick, add more hot water, a teaspoon at a time.

# GINGERBREAD CAKE DONUTS WITH HONEY GINGER ICING

I happen to be the sort of person who doesn't limit gingerbread to the holidays, and while I would eat these year-round, there is something especially festive about all those sweet, exotic spices. If you chop your own candied ginger, spray the knife with a little nonstick vegetable spray to keep the ginger pieces from sticking, and then toss the chopped ginger with a little granulated sugar to keep the pieces separate.

*Makes about 15 donuts*

12 ounces (about 3 cups) cake flour, plus more for rolling and cutting

1 tablespoon baking powder

1 teaspoon ground ginger

1 teaspoon ground cinnamon

¼ teaspoon ground cloves

¼ teaspoon ground cardamom seeds

¼ teaspoon ground nutmeg

½ teaspoon salt

4 ounces (about ½ cup) dark muscovado or dark brown sugar

1 ounce (2 tablespoons) unsalted butter at room temperature

1 large egg, at room temperature

1 large egg yolk, at room temperature

3 tablespoons dark molasses

1 teaspoon orange zest

6 tablespoons whole milk

Oil or shortening for frying

Honey Ginger Icing (see following recipe)

2 tablespoons chopped candied ginger

1. Sift the flour, baking powder, spices, and salt together in a medium bowl and set aside.

2. In a stand mixer fitted with the paddle attachment, mix the sugar and butter on low speed, until homogenous, about 1 minute. Add the egg and egg yolk, then mix on medium speed, periodically scraping the sides of the bowl with a rubber spatula, until the mixture is a couple of shades lighter, about 5 minutes. Beat in the molasses and orange zest.

3. Add the flour mixture to the beaten egg mixture in three additions, each time alternating with the milk. After each addition, mix on low speed until just combined and scrape the sides of the bowl. The dough will be very sticky, like wet cookie dough.

4. Transfer the dough to a clean bowl, press plastic wrap directly onto the dough's surface to cover, and refrigerate at least 1 hour (or up to 24 hours).

5. Using a deep fryer or a heavy pan, heat at least 2 inches of the oil or shortening to 370°F. If you're not using a deep fryer with a built-in thermostat, check the temperature using a candy or deep-fry thermometer. (See Frying Tips, p. 92.)

6. The dough is on the sticky side, so don't be afraid of using enough flour so that it doesn't stick to the work surface or the cutter. Generously flour a work surface.

Using floured hands, gently press the dough into a round about 1-inch thick. Dust the top of the dough with flour and then use a floured rolling pin to roll the dough to about ½-inch thick. Dip a 3-inch donut cutter into flour and then cut out as many circles as you can, dipping the cutter into the flour before each cut. Fold and reroll the dough to make extra donuts and cut again. You may want to refrigerate it for a few minutes to make it easier to roll. Do not reroll a third time as this will result in tough donuts.

7. Shake any excess flour off the donuts before carefully adding them to the hot fat a few at a time, taking care not to crowd them. Once the donuts float, fry for about 60 seconds per side or until deep golden brown on both sides. Drain on paper towels. Cool on a rack.

8. To ice, dip the pretty side of each cooled donut into the freshly made Honey Ginger Icing. Set icing-side up on a rack, sprinkle with the chopped ginger, and dry for 20 to 30 minutes before serving.

## HONEY GINGER ICING

*Makes about 1 cup icing, enough for about 1½ dozen donuts*

1 tablespoon grated fresh ginger
2 tablespoons warm honey
Approximately 2 tablespoons boiling water
8 ounces (about 2 cups) confectioners' sugar
¼ teaspoon salt

Put the grated ginger in a small strainer and press down to extract the juice. Measure 1 teaspoon of the juice and whisk together with the warm honey and 2 tablespoons boiling water. Gradually whisk in the sugar until all of the sugar has been incorporated. Stir in the salt. Add a little more hot water, drop by drop, if the icing seems too thick. It should cover the back of a spoon with about ⅛ inch of icing.

# KEY LIME CRULLERS

These cream-puff-pastry-based donuts are what would today be known as French crullers or what America's antebellum domestic goddess Eliza Leslie called "soft crullers." In Paris, they wouldn't have any idea what you're talking about. The crullers only became "French" in the late eighteen hundreds, roughly around the same time that fried potatoes received the same honorific. This citrusy rendition is especially light, elegant, and yummy—or should I say *délicieux*?

*Makes about 16 donuts*

1 cup water

1 tablespoon sugar

2 ounces (4 tablespoons) unsalted butter, cut into pieces

½ teaspoon salt

4½ ounces (1 cup) bleached all-purpose flour

4 large eggs

2 teaspoons lime zest (preferably Key lime)

¼ teaspoon pure lemon extract

Oil or shortening for frying

Key Lime Icing (see following recipe)

1. Make the dough: Combine the water, granulated sugar, butter, and salt in a heavy saucepan. Bring to a boil. When

the butter melts, add the flour all at once. Stir with a wooden spoon over low heat until the dough no longer sticks to the sides, about 1 minute. The dough should be soft and should not stick to your fingers.

2. Transfer the dough to a bowl. Let the dough cool 5 minutes. Add the eggs one at a time, beating until each egg is fully incorporated before adding the next. (This is best done in a heavy-duty stand mixer fitted with a paddle blade or in a food processor.) Finally, beat in the lime zest and extract. Cool to room temperature, cover with plastic wrap, and then refrigerate at least 1 hour or up to 24 hours.

3. Cut sixteen 5-inch squares of parchment paper. "Glue" these onto two baking sheets by greasing the sheets with a little butter or shortening and then adhering the parchment to the sheets. Spray the top of parchment squares lightly with nonstick cooking spray.

4. Scrape the chilled dough into a piping bag fitted with a closed ½-inch star tip. I prefer a swirl tip because it gives you that traditional French cruller swirl, but any star tip of approximately this size will work. Pipe a 3-inch ring onto each parchment square. If the end of the dough sticks to the star tip, use kitchen scissors or a paring knife to cut it free.

5. Using a deep fryer or a heavy pan, heat at least 3 inches of the oil or shortening to 350°F. If you're not using a deep fryer with a built-in thermostat, check the temperature using a candy or deep-fry thermometer. (See Frying Tips, p. 92.)

6. To fry, pick up each piece of parchment and carefully, but quickly, flip it over into the fat. Fry a few crullers at a time, making sure not to crowd them. Fry about 2 minutes per side, flipping them halfway through. If you aren't using a fryer basket, remove each cruller with a slotted spoon. Drain on several layers of paper towel. Let cool to room temperature.

7. To ice, dip the pretty side of each cooled cruller into the freshly made Key Lime Icing. Set iced-side up on a rack to dry for 20 to 30 minutes before serving.

# KEY LIME ICING

*Makes about 1 cup icing, enough to ice about 16 donuts*

¼ cup condensed milk

1 tablespoon Key lime juice

1 tablespoon boiling water

Pinch salt

6 ounces (about 1½ cups) confectioners' sugar

1 teaspoon freshly grated lime zest (preferably Key lime)

½ teaspoon pure lemon extract

Green food coloring (optional)

Combine the condensed milk, lime juice, water, and salt in a microwavable bowl. Heat in microwave until bubbling, about 15 to 30 seconds, depending on microwave. Alternately, heat ingredients in a small saucepan and then transfer to bowl. Gradually whisk in the sugar until it has been fully incorporated. Whisk in the lime zest and lemon extract. Add a little hot water, drop by drop, if the icing seems too thick. It should cover the back of a spoon with about ⅛ inch of icing. Whisk in a couple of drops of green food coloring if you wish.

# NUTELLA BOMBOLONCINI: NUTELLA-FILLED DONUT HOLES

In Florence, *bombolini* are the local take on Central European *Krapfen,* though here, as in Venice, a custard cream filling is more common than jam. The name apparently comes from *bombola,* which used to mean a round jar but eventually came to mean a gas canister. These days, *bombolone* can refer to either a family-size propane tank or a Florentine donut. I've made these smaller than your average *bombolone*—and filled them with Nutella, for no other reason than I love the stuff. There are fancier versions of the hazelnut chocolate spread first marketed by the Ferrero company, and yes, they are even more delicious. Look for them in fancy food boutiques and natural food stores.

*Makes 2 to 3 dozen*

1 cup plus 1 tablespoon lukewarm milk (about 105°F), divided

¼ ounce (1 envelope) active dry yeast

1 ounce (about 2 tablespoons) sugar, divided

1 pound plus 1½ ounces (about 4 cups) unbleached all-purpose flour

3 large egg yolks

1¾ ounces (3½ tablespoons) unsalted butter, melted and cooled, plus a little extra for brushing

1 teaspoon pure vanilla extract

141

Large pinch of salt

13-ounce jar Nutella or other hazelnut-chocolate spread

Oil or shortening for frying

Sugar for dusting

1. In a small bowl, stir together ¼ cup lukewarm milk, yeast, and 1 teaspoon sugar. Stir to dissolve. Stir in 2 ounces (about ½ cup) flour. Cover this "sponge" with plastic wrap and let rise in a warm place until doubled in volume, about 20 minutes.

2. In a separate bowl, whisk the yolks until frothy. Gradually, whisk in the melted butter and the vanilla.

3. Transfer the risen sponge to the bowl of a stand mixer fitted with the paddle attachment. On medium-low speed, beat in the egg mixture, the remainder of the milk and sugar, and then about half the flour. Switch to the dough hook attachment, gradually add the remaining flour, and finally the salt. Beat on medium-low speed until the dough is smooth, shiny, and elastic, about 5 minutes.

4. Remove the dough from the bowl and set on a floured surface. Knead very briefly to turn it into a ball. Set in a buttered bowl, cover with plastic wrap, and let rise in a warm place until doubled in volume, about 45 minutes.

5. On a floured surface, roll the dough about ½-inch thick. Using a 1¾-inch diameter cookie or biscuit cutter, cut out as many rounds as you can. Gather up the scraps and roll out the dough one more time to cut out more circles. This is easier if you let gathered-up scraps rest for 5 minutes before rerolling.

6. Brush these lightly with melted butter on each side. Set on a baking sheet lined with parchment paper and cover loosely with plastic wrap. Let rise until they are about 50 percent larger (30 to 45 minutes)—any more than that and they will expand too much during frying.

7. Using a deep fryer or a heavy pan, heat at least 2 inches of the oil or shortening to 350°F. If you're not using a deep fryer with a built-in thermostat, check the temperature using a candy or deep-fry thermometer. (See Frying Tips, p. 92.)

8. Slide the donuts into the fat one by one, making sure not to crowd the pan. Fry until both sides are light brown, about 2½ to 3 minutes, turning the donuts periodically so they brown more evenly. With a slotted spoon, lift out the cooked donuts and drain on a cooling rack set above a baking pan or on paper towels. While still warm, toss in granulated sugar. Cool to room temperature.

9. To fill the *bomboloncini*, using a small knife, make a small incision in the top center of each donut. Fill a piping bag fitted with a small star tip with the chocolate hazelnut spread. Insert the tip into the hole and pipe about 2 teaspoons in the center. Pipe a small star on the top of each donut to disguise the filling hole.

# BAKED RED VELVET DONUTS WITH VANILLA BEAN ICING

You know and I know that something that's baked in an oven is not a donut, no matter the shape. It may be delicious, as these donut-shaped cakes indeed are, but it belongs to another species. That said, the inattentive eater may well be fooled by these donut forgeries, and that presents the baker with its own sort of pleasure. You will need a pan specifically designed for this sort of subterfuge. Since the ring-shaped cakes bake so quickly, you can use the same pan for several batches. Simply wipe it out and spray again with nonstick spray.

*Makes 1 dozen*

5½ ounces (about 1⅓ cups) cake flour

1 tablespoon cocoa powder (preferably *not* Dutch processed)

½ teaspoon baking soda

½ teaspoon salt

⅓ cup buttermilk at room temperature

2 tablespoons red food coloring

½ teaspoon pure vanilla extract

½ teaspoon cider vinegar

2 ounces (¼ cup) unsalted butter, at room temperature

4 ounces (about ½ cup) sugar

1 large egg, at room temperature

Vanilla Bean Icing (see following recipe)

1. Preheat oven to 350°F. Lightly spray donut pan with vegetable spray.

2. In a small bowl, sift the flour with the cocoa powder, baking soda, and salt and set aside. In a separate small bowl, whisk together the buttermilk, red food coloring, vanilla, and cider vinegar. In the bowl of a stand mixer fitted with the paddle attachment, cream the butter and sugar until smooth and homogenous, about 2 minutes. Add the egg. Beat on medium until smooth and a couple of shades lighter, about 5 minutes.

3. Alternate between adding the buttermilk mixture and the flour mixture to the butter-and-sugar mixture in three additions. With each addition, beat until the ingredients are barely incorporated, scraping down the batter in the bowl each time. Do not overbeat or the donuts will be rubbery.

4. Using a piping bag fitted with a plain ½-inch tip or a spoon, fill each donut mold about two-thirds full, making sure the center post is clear. Bake until the donuts are light golden brown and spring back when touched, 8 to 10 minutes. Let cool slightly before removing from pan. Cool on racks to room temperature before dipping in the Vanilla Bean Icing.

5. To ice, dip the pretty side of each cooled donut into the freshly made Vanilla Bean Icing. Set icing-side up on a rack and dry for 20 to 30 minutes before serving.

# VANILLA BEAN ICING

*Makes about 1 cup icing, enough for about 1½ dozen donuts*

1 small vanilla bean

2 to 3 tablespoons boiling water

8 ounces (about 2 cups) confectioners' sugar

Using a paring knife, split the vanilla bean lengthwise and scrape out the vanilla seeds (the black interior). In a medium bowl, combine the seeds with 2 tablespoons of the boiling water, and then gradually whisk in the sugar until all of the sugar has been incorporated. Add a little more hot water, drop by drop, if the icing seems too thick. Use while still warm.

# ACKNOWLEDGMENTS

Where to begin? With the good people at the New York Public Library who provided a desk to pore over donut arcana, especially Jay Barksdale, who smoothed the way? Or with my friend Luca Colferai, who arranged my interview with Venice's storied krapfen maker, Franco Tonolo? I am grateful to them but also to many others. To Sandra Oliver for her insight into New England foodways, and to Poppy Tooker for sharing her knowledge of New Orleans; to Stephen Schmidt for calling me out on sloppy research, and to Cara De Silva for not letting me get away with lazy journalism. Then there was William Woys Weaver, the guru of all things Pennsylvania Dutch, who tolerated my ignorant queries, and Karin Vaneker, who indulged my speculation about the role of the (European) Dutch in America's donut culture. Ingrid Haslinger and Ursula Heinzelmann were both invaluable for correcting my pathetic attempts to read medieval German. Ruth Jeavons and Brendan King were terrifically useful in tracking down the likely origin of New England's donuts to Northhampshire, in no small part by getting me in touch with Dr. Heather Falvey, whose research uncovered the first donut recipe by that name. I also need to thank Mike Baxter at Belshaw and Susan Mitchem at the Salvation Army National Archives for the valuable information they provided. Tess Rose generously took the time to read the manuscript and made numerous valuable suggestions. The industrial designer Lucia N. DeRespinis gave me the inside scoop on the Dunkin' Donuts color scheme, and her daughter (my wife) tolerated months of an apartment that smelled like frying donuts. To both mother and daughter: many thanks! Finally, to my agents, Jane Dystel and Miriam Goderich, I'm ever grateful to you for doing all the stuff I'm hopelessly incompetent at.

# IMAGE CREDITS

Page vii: Courtesy of the Salvation Army National Archives

Page 6: Courtesy of Omar Zerouk

Page 7: Courtesy of Amir Moosavi

Page 9: Courtesy of Michael Krondl

Page 12: Venetian Doughnut Seller (pen & ink and w/c on paper), Grevenbroeck, Jan van (1731-1807) / Museo Correr, Venice, Italy / Giraudon / The Bridgeman Art Library

Page 19: Courtesy of Michael Krondl

Page 22: Courtesy of Lenora Genovese

Page 25: From *The Tribute Book* by Frank B. Goodrich (New York: Derby & Miller, 1865)

Page 33: Aelbert Cuyp, from the Donation Association at Dordrecht Museum

Page 36: Courtesy of Café Du Monde

Page 40: From the Crockett Collection / Camden Public Library

Page 44: Courtesy of the National Archives, Records of the Agricultural Marketing Service

Page 45: From the Gerald W. Williams Collection, Special Collections & Archives Research Center, Oregon State University

Page 48: Richards, George M. "Oh, boy! That's the girl! The Salvation Army lassie—keep her on the job." Color film copy transparency. New York: The Sackett & Wilhelms Corporation. From Library of Congress Prints and Photographs Online Catalog. http://www.loc.gov/pictures/collection/wwipos/item/2002719418/

Page 51: Photo courtesy of The Salvation Army National Archives

Page 53: "Donut eating contest, May 22, 1920." Negative glass photograph. Washington, DC: LC-DIG-npcc-06242

Page 54: Courtesy of the National Archives

Page 56: Courtesy of Library of Congress

Page 59: "U.S. soldier eating doughnuts" Photo courtesy of Library of Congress

Page 61: Photo courtesy of the Visual Instruction Department Lantern Slides, Special Collections & Archives Research Center, Oregon State University

Page 62: Courtesy of Carol M. Highsmith

Page 64: From Melissa Bunni Elian

Page 71: New York World's Fair 1939-1940 records, Manuscripts and Archives Division, The New York Public Library, Astor, Lenox and Tilden Foundations

Page 72 (above): New York World's Fair 1939-1940 records, Manuscripts and Archives Division, The New York Public Library, Astor, Lenox and Tilden Foundations

Page 72 (below): Image courtesy Belshaw Adamatic Bakery Group

Page 75: Courtesy of Dunkin' Donuts

Page 76: Courtesy of Dunkin' Donuts

Page 79: Courtesy of Tim Hortons

Page 82: Courtesy of Krispy Kreme

Page 83: Courtesy of Krispy Kreme

Page 84: Courtesy of Krispy Kreme

Page 87: Courtesy of Voodoo Doughnut

Page 88: Courtesy of Jennifer Buktaw

Pages 94–144: Recipe photos by Direct Digital Photography

# SELECTED BIBLIOGRAPHY

Abell, L. G. *The skilful housewife's book; or, Complete guide to domestic cookery, taste, comfort and economy. Embracing 659 receipts pertaining to household duties, gardening, flowers, birds, plants, etc.* New York: D. Newell, 1846.

"Advertising Introduces the Square Doughnut." *Printer's Ink.* January 15, 1920: 8,10.

Alloui, Soumia. "Algerians can't give up 'El Zalabie' during Ramadan." *EMAJ Magazine,* September 3, 2010.

*Angora Love.* Directed by Lewis R. Foster. Produced by Hal Roach. Performed by Stan Laurel and Oliver Hardy. 1929.

Arai, Juliette, Wendy Shay, and Franklin A. Robinson Jr. "Krispy Kreme Doughnut Corporation Records, ca. 1937–1997 #594. National Museum of American History, Archives Center. January 2004. http://amhistory.si.edu/archives/d7594.htm (accessed January 10, 2013).

Arundhati, P. *Royal Life in Mānasôllāsa.* New Delhi: Sundeep Prakashan, 1994.

Athenaeus of Naucratis and S. Douglas Olson. *The Deipnosophists.* Vol. VII. Cambridge, MA: Harvard University Press, 2006.

Booth, Evangeline, and Grace Livingston Hill. *The War Romance of the Salvation Army.* Philadelphia: J. B. Lippincott, 1919.

Bourgeois, David, and Josh Gillette. "Where Have All the Doughnuts Gone?" *Spy*, February 1991: 28.

Calleja, Dawn. "How Tim Hortons Will Take Over the World." *The Globe and Mail*, September 23, 2010.

Carlitz, Ruth. "Hot Doughnuts Now: The Krispy Kreme Story." *The [Duke] Chronicle*, October 22, 2003.

Catledge, Turner. "Red Cross Girls at Front Startle Doughboys in Italy." *New York Times*, January 10, 1944: 1.

——. "Without the Red Cross We'd Be Sunk." *New York Times*, February 27, 1944: SM5.

Child, Lydia Maria. *The Frugal Housewife.* Boston: Marsh and Capen, and Carter and Hendee, 1829.

Crandall, Christian S. "The Liking of Foods as a Result of Exposure: Eating Doughnuts in Alaska." *The Journal of Social Psychology* 125, no. 2 (1985): 187–194.

Dalzell, Tom. *The Routledge Dictionary of Modern American Slang and Unconventional English*. New York: Routledge, 2009.

De La Roca, Claudia. "Matt Groening Reveals the Location of the Real Springfield." *Smithsonian,* May 2012.

De Voe, Thomas F. *The Market Book, Containing a Historical Account of the Public Markets in the Cities of New York, Boston, Philadelphia and Brooklyn, With a Brief Description of Every Article of Human Food Sold Therein, The Introduction of Cattle in America, And Notices of Many Remarkable Specimens*. New York: Printed for the author, 1862.

Denison, Thomas S. "The Great Doughnut Corporation." Chicago: Denison, 1903.

"Dollars for Doughnuts." *Time*. November 11, 1940: 78.

*Dora's Dunking Doughnuts*. Directed by Harry Edwards. Performed by Shirley Temple, Andy Clyde, and Ethel Sykes. 1933.

"Doughnuts." *New York Times*. September 7, 1907: 8.

Dugan, George. "Diary Recalls Start of A.E.F. Doughnuts: Tells of the Batch and Girl That Set Them Rolling." *New York Times*, January 31, 1961: 31.

Dunkin' Donuts. "Dunkin' Donuts Press Kit." July 2012.

Edge, John T. *Donuts: An American Passion*. New York: G. P. Putnam's Sons, 2006.

Eichhoff, Jürgen. "'Ich bin ein Berliner': A History and a Linguistic Clarification." *Monatshefte* 85, no. 1 (Spring 1993): 71–80.

Emery, Sarah Smith. *Reminiscences of a Nonagenarian*. Newburyport, MA: W. H. Huse and Company, 1879.

Ephron, Nora. "Sugar Babies." *New Yorker*, February 1997: 31.

Fabricant, Florence. "Food Notes: Hanukkah Treats Grandfather's Doughnuts Dream Gelati." *New York Times*, November 23, 1994: C4.

Falvey, Heather, ed. *The Receipt Book of Baroness Elizabeth Dimsdale, c. 1800*. Hertford: Hertfordshire Record Society, 2013.

"The Feast of Doughnuts." *Baltimore Sun*. June 29, 1861: 2.

Fisher, Len. *How to Dunk a Doughnut: The Science of Everyday Life*. New York: Arcade, 2003.

Goodrich, Frank Boott. *The Tribute Book: A Record of the Munificence, Self-Sacrifice and Patriotism of the American People During the War for the Union*. New York: Derby and Miller, 1865.

Guida, Victoria. "Krispy Kreme Is Hot Stuff Once Again." *Charlotte Observer*, June 22, 2012.

Haldane, David. "A Taste of Cambodia: A Real Horatio Alger Story: Refugee Built Empire on Doughnuts." *Los Angeles Times*, December 19, 1988.

"Hanged on the Gallows: Two Men Pay the Penalty of their Crimes." *New York Times*, April 17, 1886: 2.

Hearn, Lafcadio. *La Cuisine Creole. A Collection of Culinary Recipes from Leading Chefs and Noted Creole Housewives, Who Have Made New Orleans Famous for Its Cuisine.* New York: W. H. Coleman, 1885.

Hone, William. *The Year Book, of Daily Recreation & Information Concerning Remarkable Men, Manners, Times, Seasons, Solemnities, Merry-Makings, Antiquities & Novelties, Forming a Complete History of the Year; & A Perpetual Key to the Almanac.* London: W. Tegg, 1832.

Horton, Lori, and Tim Griggs. *In Loving Memory: A Tribute to Tim Horton.* Toronto: ECW Press, 1997.

Hunter, Douglas. *Open Ice: The Tim Horton Story.* Toronto: Viking, 1994.

Irving, Washington. *The Works of Washington Irving.* Vol. VII. New York: G. P. Putnam's Sons, 1881.

Joyce, Ron, and Robert Thomson. *Always Fresh: The Untold Story of Tim Hortons by the Man Who Created a Canadian Empire.* Toronto: HarperCollins, 2006.

Kazanjian, Kirk, and Amy Joyner. *Making Dough: The 12 Secret Ingredients of Krispy Kreme's Sweet Success.* Hoboken, NJ: John Wiley and Sons, 2004.

*Küchenmeisterei.* Leipzig: Johann Beyer, 1590.

Leslie, Eliza. *Seventy-Five Receipts for Pastry, Cakes, and Sweetmeats.* Boston: Munroe and Francis, 1832.

—. *Directions for Cookery, in Its Various Branches.* Philadelphia: E. L. Carey and Hart, 1840.

—. *The Lady's Receipt-Book: A Useful Companion for Large or Small Families.* Philadelphia: Carey and Hart, 1847.

Madison, James H. *Slinging Doughnuts for the Boys: An American Woman in World War II.* Bloomington: Indiana University Press, 2007.

Maier-Bruck, Franz. *Das grosse Sacher Kochbuch: die österreichische Küche.* Munich: Sculer, 1975.

Marks, Gil. *Encyclopedia of Jewish Food.* New York: John Wiley and Sons, 2010.

McGregor, Charles. *History of the Fifteenth Regiment, New Hampshire Volunteers, 1862–1863.* Concord, NH: I. C. Evans, 1900.

Miller, William J. "'I Am a Jelly-Filled Doughnut.'" *New York Times*, April 1988: 31.

Montiño, Francisco Martínez. *Arte de cozina, pasteleria, vizcocheria y conserueria.* Madrid: Luis Sanchez, 1611.

Mullins, Paul R. *Glazed America: A History of the Doughnut*. Gainesville, FL: University Press of Florida, 2008.

Neal, John. *Brother Jonathan: or, The New Englanders*. Vol. I. Edinburgh: William Blackwood, 1825.

"News of Food: Machine Catches Up With Doughnut; It Even Can Imitate a Hand-Made One." *New York Times*. September 26, 1949: 28.

Oliver, Sandra L. *Saltwater Foodways*. Mystic, CT: Mystic Seaport Museum, 1995.

Olsen, Arthur J. "President Hailed by Over a Million in Visit to Berlin." *New York Times*, June 1963: 1.

Penfold, Steve. *The Donut: A Canadian History*. Toronto: University of Toronto Press, 2008.

Perry, Charles, trans. *An Anonymous Andalusian Cookbook of the 13th Century*. http://www.daviddfriedman.com /Medieval/Cookbooks/Andalusian/andalusian1.htm (accessed January 2013).

Quinones, Sam. "From Sweet Success to Bitter Tears." *Los Angeles Times*, January 19, 2005.

Randolph, Mary. *Virginia Housewife*. Washington, DC: Davis and Force, 1824.

Rexford, Mary Metcalfe, and Oscar Whitelaw Rexford. *Battlestars & Doughnuts: World War II Clubmobile Experiences of Mary Metcalfe Rexford*. St. Louis, MO: Patrice Press, 1989.

Rose, Peter G. *The Sensible Cook: Dutch Foodways in the Old and the New World*. Syracuse: Syracuse University Press, 1989.

Rosenberg, William, and Brilliant Keener. *Time to Make Donuts*. New York: Lebhar-Friedman Books, 2001.

"Sight of Our Men Depresses Enemy: Germans Finally Smash the Pie Cart." *New York Times*. April 5, 1918: 1.

"Salvation Army Colonel Put the Doughnut in Front Line Trenches." *Boston Daily Globe*. December 22, 1918: 21.

"The Salvation Army in World War I." The Salvation Army National Archives, n.d.

Scappi, Bartomoleo. *Opera di M. Bartolomeo Scappi, cuoco secreto di Papa Pio V diuisa in sei libri*. Venice: Michele Tramezzino, 1570.

Scheutz, Martin. "Fasching am frühneuzeitlichen Wiener Hof: Zur Domestizierung der »verkehrten Welt« in einem höfischen Umfeld." In *Wien und seine WienerInnen: Ein historischer Streifzug durch Wien über die Jahrhunderte*, by Martin Scheutz and Vlasta Valeš, 125–156. Vienna: Böhlau, 2008.

Shoemaker, Alfred Lewis. *Eastertide in Pennsylvania: A Folk-Cultural Study*. Mechanicsburg, PA: Stackpole Books, 2000.

*Springfield Daily Republican*. "The Hole in the Doughnut." March 22, 1916: 8.

Steinberg, Sally Levitt. *The Donut Book*. Pownal, VT: Storey Publishing, 2004.

Thoreau, Henry David. *Cape Cod*. Boston: Houghton, Mifflin, 1893.

Thurber, James. "The Talk of the Town, 'Glorifying the Doughnut.'" *New Yorker*, July 18, 1931: 7.

*Two Fifteenth-Century Cookery-Books*: Harleian MS. 279 (ab 1430) and Harl. MS. 4016 (ab. 1450), with extracts from Ashmole MS. 1439, Laud MS. 553, and Douce MS. 55. . London: Oxford University Press, 1964.

Van Der Sijs, Nicoline. *Cookies, Coleslaw, and Stoops: The Influence of Dutch on the North American Languages*. Amsterdam: Amsterdam University Press, 2009.

"When Everything Slows Down." *Economist*. August 14, 2010.

Whitehead, Jessup. *The Chicago Herald Cooking School: A Professional Cook's Book for Household Use, Consisting of a Series of Menus for Every Day Meals and for Private Entertainments, with Minute Instructions for Making Every Article Named*. Chicago: The author, 1883.

Winston, Diane. *Red-Hot and Righteous: The Urban Religion of the Salvation Army*. Cambridge, MA: Harvard University Press, 1999.

Young, Craig. "The Third Regiment Maine Volunteer Infantry." June 28, 2001. http://www.thirdmaine.org /PDF%20files/3rdMEshort-hist.pdf (accessed October 20, 2012).

Zenker, F. G. *Der Zuckerbäcker für Frauen mittlerer Stände. Anweisung zur leichten und wenig kostspieligen Bereitung der auserlesensten Confitüren, Kunstgebäcke, Getränke, Gefrornen &c. &c*. Vienna: C. Haas, 1834.

# INDEX